# Too Many People?

# TOO MANY PEOPLE?

**Jean F. Blashfield
and Wallace B. Black**

Educational Consultant
**Helen J. Challand, Ph.D.**
Professor of Science Education, National-Louis University

Technical Consultants
**Carl Haub** – Director, Information and Education
**Kim Crews** – Director, Population Education
Population Reference Bureau

CHILDRENS PRESS®
CHICAGO

# A production of B&B Publishing, Inc.

**Project Editor:** Jean Blashfield Black
**Designer:** Elizabeth B. Graf
**Cover Design:** Margrit Fiddle
**Artist:** Valerie A. Valusek

**Production Manager:** Dave Conant
**Photo Researcher:** Marjorie Benson
**Assistant Photo Researchers:**
   Kathy Brooks Parker
   Terri Willis

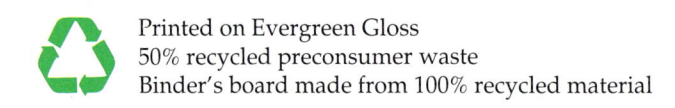

Printed on Evergreen Gloss
50% recycled preconsumer waste
Binder's board made from 100% recycled material

## Library of Congress Cataloging-in-Publication Data

Blashfield, Jean
   Too many people? / Jean F. Blashfield and Wallace B. Black
      p.  cm. -- (Saving planet earth)
   Includes index.
   ISBN 0-516-05513-5
   Summary: Presents opposing views on the effects of the earth's rising population. 1. Population--Juvenile literature. 2. Population--Environmental aspects--Juvenile literature. 3. Natural resources--Juvenile literature.
   [1. Population. 2. Natural resources.] I. Title. II. Series.
HB883.B53  1992
304.6--dc20

91-34603
CIP
AC

**Cover photo**—© Imtek Imagineering/Masterfile

Copyright © 1992 by Childrens Press®, Inc.
All rights reserved. Published simultaneously in Canada.
Printed in the United States of America.
1 2 3 4 5 6 7 8 9 10 R 00 99 98 97 96 95 94 93 92

## TABLE OF CONTENTS

| | | |
|---|---|---|
| Chapter 1 | **93 Million More People!** | 6 |
| Chapter 2 | **People Counting** | 14 |
| Chapter 3 | **Lives of Hunger, Deaths of Starvation** | 32 |
| Chapter 4 | **People versus the Environment** | 52 |
| Chapter 5 | **Family Planning** | 72 |
| Chapter 6 | **The Goal: A Sustainable Earth** | 96 |
| Chapter 7 | **Not So! – Opposing Views** | 106 |
| Chapter 8 | **Taking Action** | 114 |
| Glossary | | 122 |
| Index | | 124 |

# Chapter 1

# 93 Million More People!

IN LESS TIME THAN IT TAKES YOU to read this sentence, the population of the Earth will have grown by 15 people. Fifteen may not seem like very much, but that's more than 10,700 people an hour, 1.8 million a week, or 93 million for the year 1992. That's the equivalent of more than three Canadas! If you are reading this book in 1993 or 1994 or 1995, the population of our planet is growing even faster.

Is the number of students in your school going to grow so much that a new building will have to be constructed soon? Probably not. Most of the world's additional people are being born in what are called the "developing" countries. That means such places as Africa, South America, and parts of Asia. These nations—also called Third World countries—are already having difficulty providing the services that people need—food, education, and energy. But they are working hard to improve their people's lives and to provide jobs for them.

In the United States, the number of children born into an average family has been declining for two hundred years, except for a short-term rise. That was after fifteen years of bad times (the Great Depression and World War II). Between 1945 and 1964, 75 million children—the so-called baby boomers—were born, mainly into families that had three or four children. Since that time, the average family size has dropped again, and the growth of the U.S. population has slowed.

Even so, the United States population is increasing faster than those of the other developed countries. In fact, counting both births and immigration, it is increasing at the rate of 2.3 million people a year. The U.S. population was once

*Although water is one of the Earth's most abundant resources, it is distributed very unevenly. This farmer is fighting a losing battle as more and more land in Senegal becomes desert—unfit for growing crops and for human habitation.*

expected to level off at about 300 million near the end of the next century. But it may now reach that figure before 2025. This is due to a combination of larger immigration and a higher birth rate.

Canada's population is expected to reach its peak in the year 2026, with 31 million people. Then it will begin to fall until it eventually stabilizes at about 18 million.

## Isn't Growth Good?

Lots of people want to see an area's population increase. More people make more work for the home builders, more sales for the grocery stores, more taxes for schools, libraries, and community services, and more customers for the banks.

It makes sense to encourage population to grow if the resources are available, if there's always enough water available to support the population. But supposing the population grows during a period of abundant rain and no water shortage. What happens when a drier period comes along and the water table shrinks? Or when the lake from which water is taken comes close to drying up? Then there's trouble for everyone.

That kind of growth often happens in the United States.

It usually just means that some people have to conserve water for a while.

But if that kind of growth occurs across a whole continent such as Africa—a continent that doesn't have the water resources to grow enough food—then millions of people may starve. That's the kind of growth that many people fear is happening on our planet.

At least 1 billion people on Earth already live below the poverty level. They never have enough food to eat. They may live in a ramshackle hut. Some of the boys will probably go to school for a while, but the girls may get no education. The people kill the forests around them for firewood. Even worse, millions of children under the age of five die each year from diseases or hunger related to environmental problems.

Things don't look very good for our planet and its people.

*The parents of many of these children migrated from rural Kenya to look for a better life in the city of Nairobi. Instead, many are finding inadequate housing, unemployment, and lack of food in Nairobi's slums.*

## Talking about Numbers

The United Nations (UN) and the international organization called the World Bank regularly predict population growth. These predictions, or forecasts, are based on data obtained from the many nations of the world.

In 1989, the UN projected that the world's population would finally level off—late in the twenty-first century—at 10 billion, twice what it was in 1989. However, in 1991, the World Bank raised that estimate to 12.5 billion. Other groups feel that the estimates are still too low and that the final, stable figure will be 14 billion. A population is *stable*, or stationary, when women average about two children each so that each couple just replaces itself.

In 1950, North America and Europe (part of the regions usually referred to as "developed" or industrialized) made up one-fifth of the world's population. By 2025, those two continents will have only one-tenth of the world's people.

When the number of people increases, the size of any problem also increases. For example, in 1978 there were fewer than 5 million refugees—people who have had to leave their own country for some reason and who usually are unable to settle elsewhere. They often live in camps that turn out not to be temporary.

In 1990, there were almost 15 million refugees, including 6 million Afghans, 2 1/2 million Palestinians, almost 1 million from Mozambique, 1 million Ethiopians, and 1 million Latin Americans and Caribbeans. There may be another million people on the move at any one time because of environmental disasters, such as famine, flooding, or drought. Those big numbers represent lots of unhappy people.

*These pregnant women and their children are waiting for health care at a refugee camp in Ethiopia. Most of the mothers will not receive the care they need to have healthy infants.*

## Numbers Are People

In 1978 China decided that it would not be able to provide for all its people unless its population stopped growing so fast. Hoping to keep the population below 1.2 billion by the year 2000, the leaders decreed that new families, espe-

# If the world were a town of 1,000 people, there would be...

- 93 Europeans
- 586 Asians
- 230 illiterate
- 120 living in cardboard or tin shelters
- 500 hungry
- 250 with no wood for cooking
- 56 South Americans
- 285 with no basic medical care
- 125 Africans
- 320 with no safe water to drink
- 52 North Americans

*China suffered a severe famine in 1946 after World War II and their own civil war severely reduced food supplies. Now, the government of China is waging "war" on population growth so that the food supply will be adequate for its huge population.*

cially among the majority group called the Han, should have only one child. But then a census taken in 1990 revealed that the nation's population had already reached 1,133,682,501. A new forecast was made showing that in the year 2000 the population would probably hit 1.35 billion.

China's leaders are worried. The difference between 1.2 billion and 1.35 billion looks small when written on paper, but it represents *150,000,000* people.

In Kenya, a nation of farms, each son expects to receive a portion of his father's land to start his own farm. But Kenya's population has doubled in just 23 years. There is no way that today's sons can earn enough from their tiny, divided plots (and sadly damaged soil) to support families. More and more people are being forced off their farms and into the cities, though there is not enough work for the people who are already there.

We talk easily about the population of a country doubling, but such growth brings incredible problems. The farmers must grow twice as much food, but the amount of land available does not double. Twice as many people are using the water supplies, but there won't be more water available—in fact, the water supply is probably twice as polluted. Twice as many children must be educated, which means there must be twice as many schools built and twice as many teachers trained—or education will deteriorate for all. There could eventually be twice as many cars on the roads, with twice as many traffic jams, twice as much air pollution, and twice as much oil being transported around the world.

Throughout this book, you'll be reading lots of statistics—such as population percentages, growth rates, and billions of people. But remember, when we talk about populations, we're talking about people. It doesn't sound very important when you say that 20 percent of the population goes to bed hungry at night. But remember how many children that percentage means—hundreds of thousands more than all the children you know at school. These children have trouble sleeping because their stomachs demand food and there still won't be any when they get up in the morning. Many of them may die from lack of food. Then you will see beyond the numbers and understand what the population problem really is.

Dr. Paul Ehrlich and Anne H. Ehrlich of Stanford University call the fantastic growth of humans on Earth "the most significant terrestrial event of the past million millennia. [A millenium is 1,000 years]. No geological event in a billion years . . . has posed a threat to terrestrial life comparable to that of human overpopulation."

"The 1990s will be a critical decade," warns Nafis Sadik of the United Nations Population Fund. "The choices of the next 10 years will decide the speed of population growth for much of the next century; they will decide whether world population triples or merely doubles before it finally stops growing; they will decide whether the pace of damage to the environment speeds up or slows down."

You will be among people making choices about population—for your own sake, and for the sake of the Earth.

*In many developing countries, villagers get all their water from a common outdoor tap. These children in Bhutan are washing themselves at the community tap. Their mothers get their household water from the same tap.*

# Chapter 2

# People Counting

KNOWING HOW MANY PEOPLE LIVE in an area has always been important. Ancient societies that lived by hunting meat and gathering wild grains had to have some idea whether two wild deer or three would be needed to feed their group. In ancient Greece, leaders had to have an idea of a city's population when constructing a new outdoor theater.

Before the seventeenth century, a *census*, or count of people in an area, usually included only certain people—heads of families, people who paid taxes, and so on. Later, all the people in a town, province, or nation were counted.

The United States is required by the Constitution to conduct a census every ten years to determine how many congressional representatives each state should have. The last U.S. census was held in 1990. Other nations hold them at different times. The United Nations collects census figures from all nations of the world and forecasts, or makes projections about, how countries will grow in the coming years.

People who deal with population numbers and descriptions are called demographers. Today's demographers play an important role in planning the future growth of cities and countries. A government needs to know how big its population is, how many children it has and how old they are, and whether the population is growing or shrinking. Without such information, the wrong decisions could be made.

Private companies use demographics to sell products. Demographers know, for example, that the percentage of American people over 65 is higher than it was ten years ago. That tells a company that it might profit by advertising shampoo for white hair.

*In industrialized countries, the population over 65 is the fastest-growing group. While developed countries worry about how to take care of their aging population, developing countries worry about jobs for the young.*

15

## Earth's Changing Population

Take a look at the population graph on this page. You'll see that it goes along for many centuries with very little change until the last thousand years. Then the lines begin getting longer more quickly. Most of the growth has occurred in a very short period of time. If we had included all human history before that, the left side of the graph would have had to start even before the first page of this book!

We don't really know how many people lived on the planet before we started counting them. We can only guess, based on what we think we know about history and what we have observed about the way people live in the few remaining primitive tribes. It has been estimated that

|  |  |
|---|---|
| 1000 B.C. | 100 million |
| 1 A.D. | 200 million |
| 1650 | 500 million |
| 1800 | 1 billion |
| 1900 | 1.5 billion |
| 1930 | 2 billion |
| 1960 | 3 billion |
| 1975 | |
| 1987 | |
| 1991 | |

probably no more than 5 million people lived on the whole planet when agriculture was starting. That's not even as large as the population of metropolitan Chicago today.

The growth rate didn't always increase. For several years about 1350, the Black Death (bubonic plague), a horribly infectious disease carried by rats, spread throughout Europe. Nobody knows for sure, but probably one-fourth of the people in Europe and Asia died before the disease stopped spreading.

**The Doubling Factor.** The chart on the next page shows

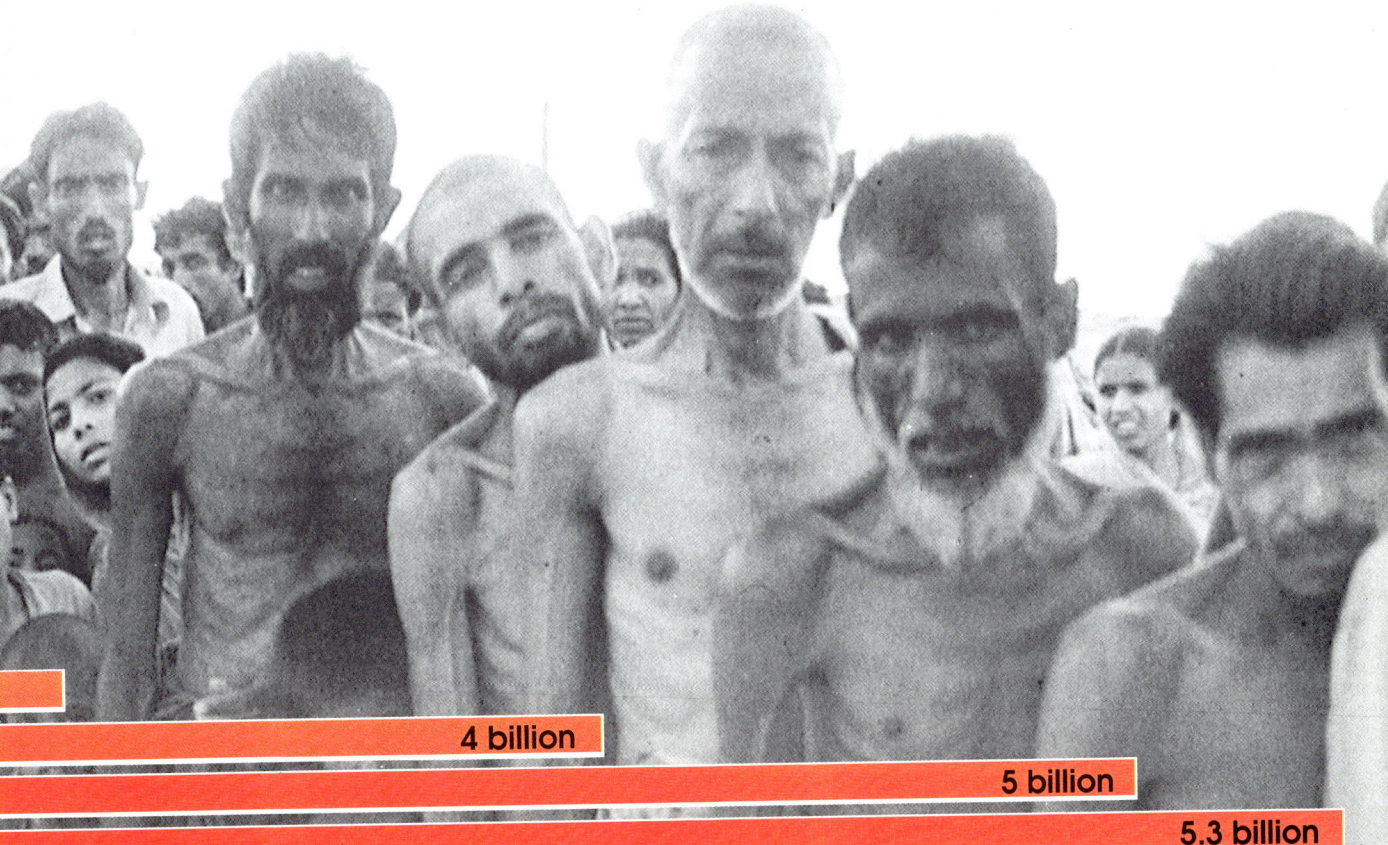

4 billion

5 billion

5.3 billion

**Earth's Population Doubling Rate**

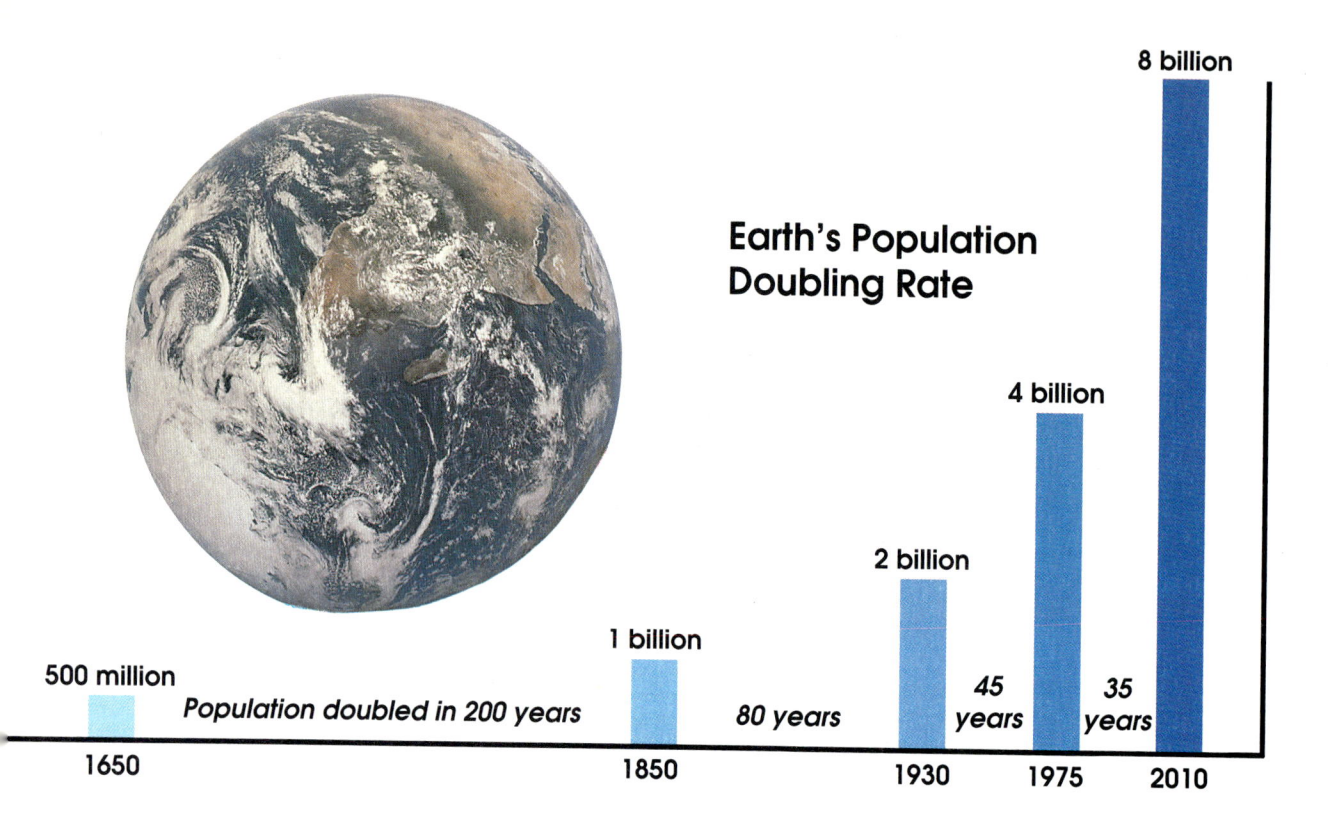

500 million — Population doubled in 200 years — 1 billion — 80 years — 2 billion — 45 years — 4 billion — 35 years — 8 billion

1650 — 1850 — 1930 — 1975 — 2010

the last 350 years more closely. Change is happening much more rapidly than it used to. The amount of time it takes for population to double is much shorter. But what does doubling matter? After all, twice something doesn't seem like very much. Try the activity at the right and see.

Or look at it this way. Suppose the population of your school doubled. There would have to be another school just as big as yours, with an equal number of desks, books, computers, and basketballs. But what if your school system didn't have enough money to build a second school right away. You might need to share your desk, locker, and books with another student. Or maybe the school would have to function in two shifts. Half of the students would go in the morning and half in the afternoon. But countries can't go on shifts of living. All of the doubled number of people are there all of the time.

## *Seeing Double*

**An Earth Experience**

*If you keep doubling the number of something you have, you still don't have very much. Right? You can find out for yourself.*

*Get a bag or jar of unpopped popcorn. Take one kernel and put it on a table. Now, double the amount you take to 2. Then take double that amount, or 4, then double that amount, or 8. How many times can you double the number you take before you run out of popcorn? Make a guess—20, 30?*

*Your final amount will depend on the size of the supply you started with, but the number of times you were able to double the popcorn pile was probably a lot lower than you estimated.*

*Earth won't run out of people the way you ran out of popcorn. But it might run out of habitable places.*

The fact that it is taking less and less time for Earth's population to double can be really dangerous to the environment. Two people sharing one locker doesn't hurt much. But imagine 10 billion people sharing space that many people think is already too crowded with 5.3 billion people. It means a lot less of everything for everyone—as well as permanent damage to the planet.

*Children at an elementary school in China*

### Rates of Change

Throughout this book we'll be using some important numbers that demographers use—birth rate, death rate, and growth rate. The actual numbers of people get very big, so it's easier to talk about the rate at which a change occurs than to describe the change itself in numbers.

The *birth rate* is the number of births per 1,000 people in a year. It is found by taking an estimate of the population at the midpoint in the year and dividing it into the number of births. If a country has an estimated midyear population of 70,000,000, and during that year 900,000 births of living children occur, the birth rate would be 900,000 ÷ 70,000,000 or 0.01286 per person, or 12.8 per 1000.

The *death rate* is figured the same way. Death rates vary widely. In many developing countries, as medical care improves, death rates go down. Good health care has increased life expectancy at birth worldwide. In developed countries, populations are aging as birth rates fall. So the death rate can actually be higher in a developed country just because the elderly are a larger group than the young. For example, Sweden's death rate is higher than Mexico's.

In Sri Lanka, the death rate from malaria dropped from 22 to 8 per 1,000 in the 25 years after World War II—just by using pesticides to kill off the disease-carrying mosquitoes.

In 1700 the average lifespan was about 25 years. (People who survived childhood, of course, usually lived longer.) It made sense in those days for teenagers to marry and have as many children as they could. In 1800, however, the average lifespan was 35 or 40. In 1900, most of the killer diseases of infants had been tackled and suddenly the average lifespan rose to 50 or even 60. But people still had large families. Populations climbed dramatically.

The *growth rate* is the birth rate minus the death rate. If a country with a birth rate of 12.8 had a death rate of 9.2, it would have a growth rate of 3.6. The closer the growth rate is to zero, the slower-growing (or more *stable*) the population is. The goal of many people who work toward reducing population growth is ZPG, or zero population growth.

The problem with the growth rate as a statistic is that the growth rate can be shrinking and yet the actual number (called the absolute number) of people it refers to can be growing. That happens because the base number of people having babies doesn't shrink. For example, a growth rate of 3.0 in a population of 5.3 billion people is 159 million people. But a growth rate of 2.0 among 8 billion people is 160 million people. The growth rate is lower, but the number of additional people is even larger.

Population also grows by immigration. Many people have immigrated to the United States, and 10 million more are expected by the year 2000. Close to a million Jews have left the former Soviet Union and migrated to Israel and other countries. This book will cover only population growth due to people having children.

Another figure that is sometimes used is the *total fertility rate*—the average number of live babies born to each woman

*Mexico's growing population and unemployment have caused many Mexicans to immigrate to the United States—legally and illegally. Here illegal immigrants cross the Rio Grande in search of a better life.*

*These children in Niger are being fed their daily ration of dry milk, some grain, and a little beef. They are the lucky ones. Many nomadic children in northern Africa are malnourished due to continuing drought.*

in her lifetime. The total fertility rate in the United States in the mid-1990s is expected to be 1.85. That rate means that couples are having fewer babies than are needed to replace themselves. The population will stabilize and go down.

Some countries, especially the industrialized nations such as the United States, Canada, Germany, and Japan, have cut their growth rates. Most of Earth's population growth is happening in the poor countries, which are called *developing countries* because they are trying to build industries that will increase the income of their growing populations. Developing nations are sometimes separated into *less* developed nations and *least* developed. Demographers predict that 95 percent of the world's population growth in coming years will take place in such countries.

## Catching Up to Ourselves

Throughout most of history, Earth's population stayed very much the same. There was a high birth rate and an equally high death rate, so the growth rate stayed close to zero. But then we started learning more about disease. More and more people moved into ways of life that were not apt to cause serious accidents. The death rate started to fall, but the birth rate stayed about the same. Therefore, the growth rate started to climb.

Gradually, as the Industrial Revolution spread, people had more money and more education. Then the birth rate began to go down, too. Eventually the birth rate and the death rate were about the same again. This time lag between reducing the death rate and then reducing the birth rate is called the *demographic transition*. It's like the momentum of a moving car. Even if you apply the brake (reduce the birth rate), it's going to take time for the car to stop.

The demographic transition took place in Western countries over the past three hundred years as they built industries and grew wealthy. When countries develop industries, many people move from rural areas to the cities. City people usually have fewer children than country people.

In developing countries, the Industrial Revolution is happening now. Many people hope that for the sake of the planet's environment, the demographic transition can be speeded up in those countries.

*Some progress is being made in developing countries to improve the industrial base. Here, aluminum ingots produced in Ghana are being loaded for shipment to other countries.*

But if we're catching up with the time lag, why are people so worried about population growth?

The big problem right now is that 33 percent of the population in developing countries is below the age of 15. In Africa alone it's almost 50 percent. All those billions of young people have their child-bearing years ahead of them. So although the birth rate may be going down, the absolute number of people having children is huge.

If each couple just replaced themselves—by having only two children—there would be no problem. But it's natural for men and women to have sexual intercourse. And when they do, chances are that sooner or later the women will get pregnant. Women in many African nations may produce between six and eight living children.

The demographic transition may take another fifty years in developing countries. By that time, the Earth may not be able to support the large number of people using its resources.

Major forecasts of population for the next century predict that most countries will reach their highest level about 2050 and then begin to decline slightly to a figure that should remain stable. But demographers don't put a lot of faith in long-range forecasts.

*The Zulus of South Africa practice polygamy (having more than one mate). The three women above are married to the same man. His wealth is measured by how large his family is.*

## How We've Looked at Population

Thomas R. Malthus was a British clergyman and university professor who published a paper in 1798 called *An Essay on the Principle of Population as it Affects the Future Improvement of Society.* In it, he described what is still regarded by many people as the basic problem with population growth.

Malthus said that unless something happens to slow it, population grows by geometric progression. That means that it continually doubles: 1, 2, 4, 8, 16, 32, 64, and so on. But he thought that the means of feeding people increases by arithmetic progression: 1, 2, 3, 4, 5, 6, 7, 8. Because of this inequality, Malthus said that people are destined to reach a bare subsistence level—they would have just enough to stay alive but no more. Life would be kept at subsistence level by war, famine, and disease.

Malthus thought that whenever a new baby is born, the living standard of its family—and its whole society—goes down because more people have to share the same amount of resources. Therefore, if the population is allowed to keep growing, everyone eventually ends up in poverty.

Malthus's ideas were quickly taken up by many different people, who formed Malthusian Leagues to try to get people to limit population growth. They believed that human populations would grow faster than Earth could support them.

---

**J. H. Fremlin, a British physicist, figured out from the amount of heat the human body gives off that the theoretical limit to the number of people who could live on Earth was 60 quadrillion. That would be 1 person for every 13 square inches (84.5 square centimeters) of space. Any more than that and the heat given off would be too great to dissipate into space. He figured that people would live in skyscrapers 2,000 stories high.**

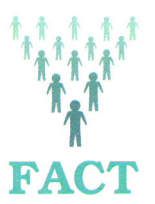

FACT

**A New Look at the Population Explosion.** In 1968, Dr. Paul Ehrlich published a book called *The Population Bomb*. In it, he came to much the same conclusions as Malthus, but his ideas were based on the whole planet, not just food supplies.

This was a new idea for many people not yet aware that human activity was hurting the environment. In 1970, when the first Earth Day was held, speakers everywhere pointed out the importance of reducing population growth if we were going to survive on Earth. But between Earth Day 1970 and Earth Day 1990, Earth's population grew by 45 percent.

In 1972, a group of businessmen and professors called the Club of Rome published *The Limits to Growth*. At that time, the Middle East oil countries were holding back oil, making it seem as if natural resources were running out.

A few years later, President Jimmy Carter issued a report called *Global 2000 Report to the President of the United States*. It, too, warned of dire things happening to the Earth because of overpopulation, wasting resources, and continued pollution.

**But It Isn't Happening.** Soon, though, many people began to look closely at what was happening on Earth and realized that people appeared to be living better than they ever had.

A 1986 report from the National Academy of Sciences observed that the world's people were better off than they had been thirty years earlier, even though the world's population had risen. Fewer people were starving to death. Average income in the Third World had increased. Prices of natural resources had dropped—instead of rising as predicted.

It appeared that population growth was not such a bad thing after all. In fact, it might even be good. We'll learn more about this view of population growth in Chapter 7.

*The African nation of Gabon was covered with thick tropical forests, but the demand for okoume and mahogany logs has destroyed this precious natural resource.*

**"Why isn't everyone as scared as we are?"** Paul Ehrlich and his wife, Anne H. Ehrlich, asked that question in their 1990 book, *The Population Explosion.* They looked at the world around them and saw that while people were, indeed, earning more money, the Earth itself was in trouble.

The burning of fossil fuels—coal, oil, and natural gas—was putting pollutants into the atmosphere that were making the temperature of the whole planet increase in a process called *global warming.* The destruction of huge, irreplaceable forests is contributing to global warming, as well as to the loss of many species of plants and animals along with precious topsoil. The growing number of cars on our roads put pollutants into the air that make smog, which harms our breathing and damages our crops. The growing use of industrial chemicals and fertilizers poisons our water supplies.

All in all, the Ehrlichs say, the planet is continuing to look more unhealthy as the human population gets bigger.

With 93 million new people each year—and 95 percent of them in Third World countries—the developing countries need to create many millions of new jobs—at least 1.4 billion of them by 2025. But these countries don't have work for the people who already need jobs. To produce new jobs, they have to start building industries to employ people.

Unfortunately, the cheapest way to establish new industries is to power them with cheap fuels, especially coal. And burning coal to produce electricity is the main culprit in pollution of the atmosphere. Also, as these nations industrialize, more and more people are going to want cars, refrigerators, and all the other things that people in Western

## An Earth Experience

### No Room to Play

*With the help of your teacher set up a recess period that will give your classmates something to think about. It has to do with the number of people and the size of their country. This activity will test your math skills.*

*Select three developed countries, such as the United States, Japan, France, Australia, or Canada. Research in the school library to find out the population of each country and its size in square miles (or square kilometers). Do the same for three developing nations, such as India, Algeria, and Indonesia.*

*Add up the population for each group. What is the total number of people in all the countries you picked? What percent lives in the Third World countries? What percent lives in the developed countries?*

*Divide your classmates by the same two percentages. It is estimated that 75 percent of the people in the world live in a developing country. If you came close to this figure with a class of, say, 29, you would have 7 living in developed countries and 22 in developing countries.*

nations take for granted. This growth will add to global warming and other pollution.

## Population and the Environment

The idea that population and environment are completely interrelated is not new. Humans developed as part of the environment, and it has always played an absolutely unavoidable part in our lives, just as it does in the lives of other living things.

We need air to breathe, water to drink, and food to eat.

*Next take the square miles for each country and repeat the process. What percent of the total makes up each of the two groups?*

*Measure the size of the playground you will use for recess. Divide it into two sections with the percentages of square miles you figured. During recess, each group can play only in its designated area. Most of the playground equipment should be in the section for the developed nations. They have 83 percent of the world's money, over 90 percent of the industry, and consume 85 percent of the world's energy. Therefore the equipment belongs to the few students playing in this group.*

*After recess, return to the classroom and discuss how it felt to be in one section or the other.*

*Life is very difficult for women in developing nations. These Ethiopian women must get their daily water supply from a common tap and then haul it back to their homes on their backs.*

As clever as humans are, we have not yet figured out how to get those three things without involving Earth.

In the old days of rural living, couples did not get married until the harvest was in. Then, if the harvest hadn't been good, they probably would not marry. Or if they married, they deliberately did not have children.

It seems unthinkable to us, but in some parts of the world—and not that long ago—some parents sold their children when they were in danger of starving. This was still done in this century. If parents couldn't sell their children in the hope of getting them into a place where food might be available, they sometimes killed them to save them from suffering starvation.

Basically, though, having children was always regarded as a good thing. The number of children who died in infancy was very high—and still is in many developing countries. As recently as 1965, for example, infant mortality (the death rate among children under 1 year old) was 125 out of 1,000. If a family wanted to be sure to have some children survive into adulthood, they kept on having babies. On farms, children were needed to help do the work. Even a three- or four-year-old could help by watching the cows. When the children were grown, they were expected to support the parents.

Many African women spend much of their day working their small fields and gathering wood for fuel. For them, it makes sense to have many children because there will be more hands to help them in their endless tasks. Twenty-four of the 42 countries with population growth rates above 3 are in Africa. In Kenya, until recently, the average woman produced 8.1 children. Today the number is down to 6.7.

Families in industrial societies do not need so many children. In fact, large families can be a problem. Housing is more expensive and children can't earn a living until they are grown. But in the Third World, even the city populations continue to rise at an alarming rate.

## Overcrowded Land

**An Earth Experience**

*The United States Census for 1990 provided the following data. You will need to supply the figures for your hometown.*

|  | Population | Size in Square Miles |
|---|---|---|
| Los Angeles | 3,485,398 | 470 |
| Chicago | 2,783,726 | 228 |
| Boston | 574,283 | 47 |
| Your town | ? | ? |

*Assume that a "typical" family of four lives in a house on a 1/4-acre lot. There are 640 acres in a square mile. Figure out the solutions to these problems:*

*If every family in the four cities above (including yours) lived in a "typical" home, what would the population be?*

*Now take the actual population of each city and calculate the space that would be allotted to each person if the land were equally divided. Don't forget that each person would have to give up a portion of his/her share for all the structures in the city besides houses and apartment buildings.*

*Is owning a house and yard—an "American Dream"—a realistic and attainable goal for most families in a big city?*

# Chapter 3

# Lives of Hunger, Deaths of Starvation

A SMALL CHILD IS CARRIED by his mother as she stumbles into the camp. He is too weak to walk. Although he is about three years old, his body looks like that of a very thin one-year-old. His face looks ancient.

The boy and his mother are not refugees fleeing a war or a bad political situation. They are refugees in their own land. Lack of rain has ruined the crops for several years, and there isn't enough food for all the people. The boy's little sister has already died, and his mother is frightened because she is expecting another baby. The boy and his mother have had to leave his father and older brothers and sisters to come to this food-distribution center. Here, they hope to get enough milk and cereal to keep them alive.

The boy and his mother are "lucky." They will be kept from starving to death—this time.

Other children are not so lucky. The United Nations estimates that 40,000 children die of starvation every year.

## Starvation and Hunger

When people do not get enough food regularly for long periods of time, the body takes the food it needs for energy from the existing tissues. Starving people gradually waste away, until the organs stop functioning.

**Up to one-third of all deaths worldwide are caused by the lack of proper foods. Many people who die of disease or dehydration (water loss) would probably have been able to fight off the additional problem if they had been properly fed.**

FACT

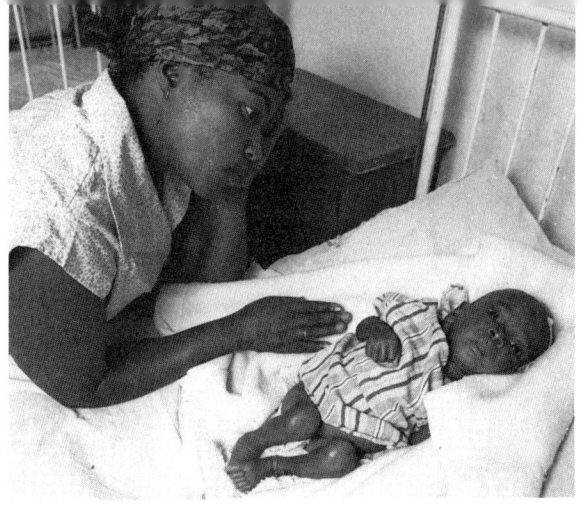

*A disease called kwashiorkor (malnourishment) is a common cause of death for children in Africa (right) and Asia. In many developing countries, such as Bangladesh (left), people believe that having lots of children is necessary since many die during childhood.*

In some societies as many as one-fourth of all the children die before they reach the age of five. In a famine year, that number may increase. Therefore, many families feel that large numbers of children are the only way to be sure that some will survive to take care of the parents in their old age.

In a household that does not have enough to eat, the women are often the last to get food. And yet a pregnant woman needs more protein than any other adult for the baby that is developing inside of her to grow properly. If the baby doesn't get the food it needs, it is already malnourished when it is born.

**Malnourishment.** Children may suffer from malnourishment, or improper nutrition, even when they seem to be getting enough to eat. In much of Africa, for example, if certain elements are missing from the diet for too long, a child may develop a disease called kwashiorkor. One symptom is a bloated stomach that makes the child look fat when it is actually malnourished.

The name is said to mean "the sickness the child develops when another baby is born." The Ghanaians called it that because the condition is often seen in children between one and two years old—about the time that a new baby may be born into the family. But it has nothing to do with the new baby. It strikes children who do not get enough protein. Children go from mother's milk to eating only cassava, potatoes, and other starchy foods, just when they need a lot of protein to grow on.

Many more children—perhaps a third of all the children in the world—get only a little less food than they need. A child grows to one-fifth of its adult size before age three, but its brain grows to four-fifths adult size in that same period. That growth depends on enough protein in the diet. The child may survive famine and later get enough protein, but by then the damage is done. The child will never have the full intelligence or size that it should have had.

## *Full But Starving*

*Some children live on a cup or two of rice a day. They may not be actively hungry, but they are malnourished. Let's see what this kind of limited diet will do to plants.*

*Mix equal amounts of sand, gravel, and cooked rice. Fill pot #1 with this "soil." Fill pot #2 with just sand and gravel. Plant several corn or wheat seeds in each pot. Water pot #1 with tap water. Water the second pot with water that has plant food added. Follow the directions on the box of plant food for the amount to be mixed with a quart of water. Commercial plant food has all the minerals and nutrients needed for healthy growth.*

*Keep careful records of how long it takes the seeds to germinate and how the plants grow in the different pots. Rice is nice, but does a diet of rice alone have enough nutrition to grow healthy plants?*

# An Earth Experience

Malnourished adults usually cut back on activity to conserve energy. When they are not working, they may appear to just lie around. They may not die, but they cannot do all they would like. First they let their homes deteriorate. Then they spend less effort taking care of their families. Finally they may not even be able to work to earn money for food. If nothing is done to change the way they live, real starvation will set in.

Hunger and stunted growth are widespread—and not just in underdeveloped countries. Even in highly industrialized countries such as the United States, it is estimated that 10 percent of all people are malnourished.

## The Problems with Farming

The three most important foods in the world are grasses—wheat, corn, and rice, and the most important is rice. It is the main food for more than half the world's population, close to 3 billion people. Fortunately, rice grows well in tropical countries, unlike wheat, the world's second main crop. China grows the most rice, the Soviet republics grow the most wheat, and the United States grows the most corn.

North America has some of the best farmland in the

*These children are victims of the continuing drought in Ethiopia. Suffering from malnutrition, many children are close to fatal starvation.*

world, and its weather is fairly reliable. These conditions help produce the best crops anywhere in the world, usually more than our own nations need. Much of the rest of the world isn't so lucky.

**Water for Crops.** Parts of Asia and much of Africa have monsoons—major wind systems that change their direction twice each year. During the summer, the monsoons bring vast quantities of water to these lands. The problem is that the monsoon isn't always as dependable as it should be. Some summers the rains don't come. The soil cracks in the drought and plants shrivel up. In other summers, the wind brings so much rain that the land floods and becomes waterlogged. Again, the crops don't grow.

The amount of farmland that is irrigated varies greatly from country to country. India irrigates only about one-third of its farmland, but that adds up to the largest amount of irrigated land of any nation in the world—approximately 136 million acres (55 million hectares). Egypt, on the other hand, irrigates all its cropland—8 million acres (3.2 million hectares). The United States, with 47 million acres (19 million hectares) of farmland, irrigates only about 10 percent. In all, about 17 percent of the world's farmland is irrigated, but

*Dead cows litter this drought-stricken area of Senegal* (left). *In an effort to become less dependent on irregular monsoons, Morocco has built dams for irrigation to ensure a more constant water supply for its rice paddies* (right).

*The topsoil in much of Mexico's Yucatán Peninsula is only 6 inches (15 centimeters) deep. Once vegetation is cleared, this precious soil is often washed away, exposing rock, and the land becomes useless and unproductive.*

that 17 percent produces a third of the world's food.

New land is not being irrigated nearly fast enough to keep up with the population increase. In Africa, where irrigation is most needed, the cost of building irrigation projects is too high. Before they build dams and other irrigation equipment, they have to build roads into the worksites. And Africa has no big tracts of usable land that justify the cost.

In addition, few other regions have the fertile topsoil of

## An Earth Experience

### Growing Food Isn't Easy

In many Third World countries, land and weather conditions produce problems for growing crops. Poor soil, drought, and monsoons make it difficult to provide food for the millions of people that need to be fed. Conduct the following two experiments to see these effects firsthand.

Select a variety of seeds that are planted as food crops, such as corn, wheat, millet, and sorghum. Locate six large wooden boxes or planters. Fill three of them, each with a different type of soil: sand in #1, clay in #2, and loam in #3. Plant the seeds according to the directions on the packages. Provide the same amount of water, warmth, and sunlight for all planters. Record the time it takes the

North America. In many parts of the world, the soil contains lots of sand or few nutrients. To make crops grow well, the farmers in such regions often have to add fertilizer, which costs a lot.

Much of the world exists on what is called subsistence farming, which means that even by working very hard, a farmer can produce only enough food to feed his own family. If the slightest thing goes wrong, his family goes hungry.

Right now, 55 countries that depend on subsistence farming are unable to feed their people. By the year 2000, another 10 nations are expected to join the list. In all these countries, the population is growing rapidly. If they can't feed their people now, how will they be able to in the future?

Oddly enough, many countries now regarded as underdeveloped actually grew so much grain before World War II that they were able to export it. The money from exports

---

*seeds to germinate, and note the height, color, and number of leaves on each plant. The only variable should be the soil type. What can you conclude?*

*For the second experiment, use the same kinds of seeds, but this time plant them in the same good soil. The variable will be the amount of water given each of the three planters. In #4, water the plants as soon as the surface dries out. That planter will be your control. Water planter #5 each day to simulate the monsoon season. Planter #6 should illustrate drought conditions—just give it a little water every couple of weeks.*

*Record the results after one month. Draw conclusions. Find out which countries have too much or too little rain. Do they have a problem producing enough food for their growing population?*

provided cash to spend on other things, such as education, culture, and city cleanup. Now, those same countries have so many people that they must import grain to feed them.

Where is the food going to come from to feed all the new people, when the world isn't doing such a hot job of feeding the ones we've got?

The amount of land that can be used for farming may rise a little by the year 2000—perhaps 5 percent. But that won't be enough to handle the additional people born during those years. If there is to be enough additional food, it must come from increased productivity. But increased productivity requires additional water, fertilizer, and other chemicals.

## The Green Revolution

Back in the 1960s, the Ford Foundation and the Rockefeller Foundation supported research into agriculture. The object was to increase the yields of the main grain plants (rice, wheat, corn, barley, and millet) by breeding special seeds and using increased irrigation and fertilizers. They were successful in breeding smaller plants that produced more grain and were more resistant to diseases and insects.

These "miracle" seeds were distributed throughout the Third World countries, and the Green Revolution began. In Latin America and Asia, the yields of rice and wheat doubled, tripled, and even quadrupled during the 1970s. Africa was not so lucky because it does not have the water resources to provide the irrigation that these plants required.

Because of the Green Revolution, such countries as Indonesia and India, which used to import food, can now survive on their own grain supplies. In fact, India even manages to export some to other countries. In 1987, India had a terrible

By the late 1960s, most corn grown in the United States was genetically uniform. Using hybrid seeds made growing corn more efficient, and easier to harvest and process (top left). Hybrid seeds were developed so that crop yields would be high. Vegetables and fruits were bred to be uniform in size and ripen at the same time (top right). Crops could be harvested by machines and transported long distances without spoiling. Different strains of hybrid rice developed for Third World countries allowed many countries such as the Philippines (right) and India to feed their populations. But due to the excessive use of pesticides (bottom right) and the genetic uniformity of hybrid seeds, many pests and plant diseases have become resistant to pesticides. As farmers rely more and more on fertilizers (bottom left), pesticides, and irrigation, yields of rice and wheat have fallen, and soil and water pollution have become major problems.

drought, which once would have meant famine. But because it had improved its grain production in recent years, India had enough to feed the hungry people.

Between 1950 and 1984, food production of the world multiplied by 2.4 times. During that same time, the population of the Earth doubled. Since 1986, however, the food supply has started to go down in relation to population. The gains from the Green Revolution seem to be over. In fact, it has created problems.

**The Green Problem with Pests.** Farmers in Sri Lanka used to grow about 2,000 varieties of rice, most of them developed by farmers for use in their specific settings. Now, however, the Green Revolution has caused them to replace their varieties with only five specialized hybrids.

Many plant scientists regard the loss of varieties and species—called gene erosion—as a dangerous thing. The miracle plants were hybridized to withstand certain diseases and pests. But diseases and pests can change, too. A disease might develop that the Green Revolution plants couldn't resist. Famine would follow.

Before the Green Revolution, a particular pest or disease would have been able to attack only one or two varieties, and the damage would not have been widespread. Now, it could be devastating.

In 1970, perhaps 15 percent of the United States crop of corn was damaged by one species of corn-leaf blight. That amount was enough to hurt the food reserves of the world. If many different varieties of corn had been planted across the country instead of just a few, the crop would not have been harmed so badly.

During the 1800s, nearly a million people in Ireland starved to death because their genetically identical potato crop was killed by a single species of invading fungus. Another million Irish people immigrated to the United States, increasing its population.

In many rice-growing regions, the people get a great deal of their protein from shrimp and fish that grow in the water of the rice paddies. But insecticides used to protect the rice crop have poisoned that water, killing the protein crop. In addition, increased use of pesticides in some countries has caused the native insects to become increasingly resistant to the poisons.

**The Green Problem with Water.** Green Revolution crops needed a great deal of water. Food supplies depend on water supplies, both normal rainfall and extra water for irrigation. As the population grows and more food is needed, additional water is needed. But there may not be any.

Some countries can produce two, or even three, crops per year on land that is now producing just one. But the crops would have to be irrigated, raising the farmers' costs.

*Ghana's Volta Dam provides valuable water and power supplies (left). Water projects have allowed some farmers, such as this one from Zambia (right), to escape subsistence farming. By irrigating, they are able to produce vegetables to sell.*

Big water projects cost a great deal of money, and they often do great damage to other aspects of the environment—a concern that people are being very vocal about now. Large-scale water projects often disrupt the lives of many subsistence farmers, while benefiting only a few.

**FACT**

It takes 2 ½ times as much water to irrigate fields that are being used to grow sugarcane as it does to irrigate fields growing wheat. But the people in developed countries demand that sugarcane be grown because we like foods to be sweet.

**The Green Problem with Fertilizers.** During the Green Revolution, land that wasn't really very good was often put into production. The nutrients it contained are now gone, and in addition, irrigation has made the land erode. Chemical fertilizers have damaged it.

When fertilizer runs out of soil in irrigation or rainwater, it collects in rivers and lakes. The nutrients in it feed algae, water hyacinths, and other abundant plants, which gradually cover the water's surface. That growth keeps sunlight out of the water, and other plants and animals begin to disappear. Fertilizers, combined with poisons from pesticides, can gradually destroy water resources.

**The Green Problem with Energy.** Instead of using only the sun and human muscle power to grow crops, our modern farmers use considerable fossil fuel.

Fuel is burned to run pumps that send irrigation water into the fields. Fuel is burned to produce fertilizers and pesticides. Fuel is burned to run tractors and combines and harvesters, and fuel is burned to carry the crops to market. In fact, it costs more power, in terms of calories (units of heat), to produce a crop than the crop itself provides for people.

Norman Borlaug is an Iowa scientist who won the 1970 Nobel Peace Prize for pioneering the Green Revolution. He insists that the growth in food supplies during the last 50 years may not continue. Crop production leveled off in the 1980s and will probably drop from now on, just when "the population monster," as he calls the problem, worsens.

## The Lands with Too Much

Robert and Leona Train Rienow in *Moment in the Sun* said that each American baby was born screaming for "26,000,000 tons of water, 21,000 gallons of gasoline, 10,150 pounds of meat, 28,000 pounds of milk and cream, 9,000 pounds of wheat, and great storehouses of all other foods, drinks, and tobaccos. These are the lifetime demands of his country and its economy."

People in the United States and other nations, who are often called the "haves," use more food than people in most other areas of the Earth. Most of us waste almost as much as we eat—letting food spoil in refrigerators, leaving food in restaurants, and even, in the past, burning surplus crops.

*China still relies on muscle power to plant and harvest many of its crops* (right). *But most industrialized nations use huge amounts of fossil fuels to grow, harvest, and transport crops to market* (left).

## An Earth Experience

### *The Cost of Eating*

*In India, the average family of eight lives on $1,200 a year. What does it cost your family for necessities for one year?*

*With the help of your parent(s), figure out how much your family spent for a full year. Include rent or house payments, utilities, clothes, transportation costs, insurance payments, entertainment, food, health care, household items, recreation, etc. Total up each category separately. What percent of the total goes for food?*

*In wealthy countries such as the United States, families spend 20 to 25 percent of their annual budget on food. In the poorest countries, such as Afghanistan and Ethiopia, a family spends 75 to 80 percent of its income on food. Even then their diet may be high in calories but low in protein, fruits, or vegetables.*

*Let's pretend that you live in one of those countries. Figure out 75 percent of your total budget. This amount must be used for food to stay alive. You must reduce all costs other than food down to 25 percent of your total budget. Which items in your current budget can you eliminate? Such choices can be very difficult. Discuss the problem with your family or classmates.*

**Feeding Cattle So We Can Eat.** Frances Moore Lappé, the author of *Diet for a Small Planet,* introduced many Americans to some of the facts that we had traditionally ignored about food. Most of us, for example, grew up believing that we had to have meat at most meals or we wouldn't get enough protein. Actually, most of us get too much protein—more than our bodies need. And the kinds of protein we need are obtainable by eating various grains in combinations.

We feed 16 pounds (7.3 kilograms) of grain and soybeans

to a cow and in return we get only 1 pound (0.4 kilogram) of beef. But to grow the grain and soybeans, we used fertilizer, pesticides, labor, and probably irrigation water. The 1 pound of beef uses up 2,500 gallons (9,463 liters) of water. It also takes 40 times as much energy value in fossil fuels to create the energy value in the pound of beef.

In a food chain, the first level—plants, or *producers*—acquires energy from the sun and produces food by photosynthesis. The second level consists of *primary consumers*—those animals that eat plants. Humans are primary consumers when they eat grains and vegetables. However, the plants may be fed to cattle or pigs, which are then primary consumers. Humans eat the beef from the cattle and become *secondary consumers.* Little of the original energy is left.

Sure it's nice to have beef and other meats once in a while, but we certainly don't need them as the basic ingredient in our diets, and for the sake of the world's agriculture,

*From Argentina* (left) *to the Sudan* (right) *in Africa, cattle require huge amounts of the Earth's natural resources. If humans would cut down on their desire for meat, valuable forests, land, and water would be saved.*

it's probably better that we don't rely on them for our proteins. The lower we can eat on the food chain (by eating plants directly), the healthier for the planet.

Of course, food also comes from the sea. More than half of the people of Africa, for example, depend on fish for much of their protein. However, the seas are being polluted by the "have" countries, so that while the world's populations of people are rising, its populations of fish are declining.

**An Earth Experience**

## *Waste Not, Want Not*

*A school cafeteria, a dedicated teacher, and a class of students concerned about the environment are required for this activity. It involves measuring wasted food and developing a program to reduce the problem.*

*Divide the class into teams to collect the leftover food on students' plates near each disposal basket in the cafeteria. Weigh the container that will be used to collect the waste. At the end of the lunch period weigh the container again and subtract the weight of the container. How many pounds of food each day become garbage? Also keep a record for a week of the kinds of food that are discarded. Give this information to the dietitian planning the daily menus.*

*Plan a program to educate all students. Encourage everyone to conduct the same experiment at home. Be sure to include the food that spoils in the refrigerator and has to be thrown away. Promote the composting of wasted food rather than sending it to a landfill. Suggest taking smaller helpings, and saving or sharing food.*

*Put posters around the school giving facts about world hunger. For example, 14 million children in Nigeria, 33 million in Indonesia, and 200 million in India do not get enough food.*

The United Nations Food and Agriculture Organization says that every person on Earth could have 3,600 calories a day in grains if there were some way to get the food distributed. That is more than enough for an adequate diet.

**FACT**

## Meeting the Needs of Developing Countries

The amount of food available is not the only problem for countries with growing populations. Throughout the world there are difficulties related to food that have to do with social problems.

**Getting Food to Where It's Needed.** Sometimes food distribution is the cause of hunger. Food for all the people in a large city cannot be grown close to the city. It has to come from far away. Transportation immediately raises the cost of the food, limiting the number of people it reaches.

People may go hungry because of social inequality. The wealthier people are able to buy more of the available food, leaving less for the poor. The government may make less effort to distribute food to the poorer people.

**The Need for Cash.** In the first half of the 1980s, the production of grains fell around the world. The number of people going hungry, even starving, increased. That means these nations must buy food

*Many Latin American countries rely on huge open markets such as this one in Guayaquil, Ecuador, to supply food for their growing urban populations. Although food may be available, it is often polluted or too expensive for the city's poor.*

from other countries. To get the money, they must increase their industrial development. Some countries cut down hardwood trees to bring in cash. But what will they do when these natural treasures are gone?

World observers project that by the year 2000, these countries will have to import up to 132 million tons (119 million metric tons) of food each year. And yet they don't have the cash to pay for all this food.

The need for cash sometimes controls the kind of food people eat in various countries. For example, North Americans are fond of shrimp, which grow along the coasts of many countries. Because North America is willing to pay for shrimp, people in these countries harvest the crustaceans and sell them. Here, the shrimp are something nice to eat. But in the countries where shrimp grow, the shrimp could provide vital protein to their own starving citizens.

## Hunger and Power

There are reports that Ethiopia has starved some of its citizens, especially those opposed to the government in power, by not distributing food in certain areas. In the 1930s, the leaders of the Soviet Union deliberately starved several million people in the Ukraine, who had long objected to Communist rule. In 1991, the Ukraine was one of the first

*Food distributed through a United Nations relief program helps nursing mothers in Bhutan* (left) *receive some needed protein. Getting food where it is needed is a worldwide problem. These Haitians are waiting for trucks to transport grain to market* (right).

republics to try to separate from the Soviet Union.

Those are extreme examples of what Frances Moore Lappé means when she says that the problem is not too little food but that food—from planting to distribution—is controlled by people with power. In a family, a woman may not have enough power to get her fair share of the available food. On a continent like South America, the ownership of land is in the hands of a few wealthy people who have power.

And most important, the poor in developing countries lack the power to change their lives. Even when other nations set up programs such as irrigation projects to improve their conditions, the people with the power in the area somehow end up controlling the improvements.

Lappé claims that even in the United States, productive farmland is under the control of fewer and fewer people. The control of food processing is also becoming tighter, which makes prices increase. She says that we pay billions of dollars more each year for food because food production is concentrated in the hands of a few companies.

A recent Worldwatch Institute report said that the poorest countries, such as Ethiopia and Nigeria, cannot feed their growing number of people. Therefore, their populations will probably be reduced by starvation. The report predicted: "Either these societies will move quickly to encourage smaller families and bring birth rates down, or rising death rates from hunger and malnutrition will check population growth."

In 1798, Thomas Malthus said, "The power of population is infinitely greater than the power in the earth to produce subsistence for man." Can we prove him wrong, without destroying the environment?

# Chapter 4
# People versus the Environment

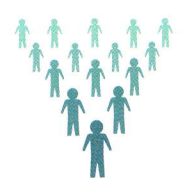

THE CHILDREN CROWDED into the little cardboard shack that their father had built in the slums of São Paulo, Brazil. It was raining outside, but they were luckier than some of their neighbors because their "house" at least had some plastic sheeting over the top to keep the rain from dissolving the cardboard walls. The oldest boy had found the plastic a few days earlier when he was rummaging through the city dump. He would rather have been at school, but he knew he had to help the family while his father looked for work.

Maybe his father could go back to farming now, the boy thought excitedly. He was the only one of the kids to remember when the family lived on a farm. They had been forced to leave when the owners of the land decided they wanted it for something else. His father had not found work in the city. What little money the family had came from his mother cleaning an office building. But she wasn't very strong since the last baby was born.

As he tried to stop the squabble between his two little sisters, who wanted more room to play, he dreamed about moving. The government was giving his family a section of Amazon rain forest to turn into a farm. He knew that he and his father would have to work hard to clear the land, but he was big enough to do it. Maybe finally their dream would come true.

When the number of people living along the Atlantic coast of Brazil became too big for the cities to hold, the Brazilian government offered many families land in

*Many Colombian children survive amid the trash heaps of urban Bogotá. To survive, they sift through the trash searching for things they might be able to sell.*

*Members of two families of subsistence farmers stand outside the house of one of the farmers in Brazil. Hoping for a better life away from the city, they cleared land, but the land wasn't fertile enough to support good crops for more than a year or two.*

the jungle. All they had to do was clear the rain forest to make a small farm. But often their dreams turned to dust. The land beneath the jungle trees was not fertile enough to support crops for more than a year or two. And the people did not have the money to buy fertilizers. With the trees gone, the exposed soil was washed away when it rained.

The people moved to another plot of land, cleared more forest, and tried again. In this way, thousands of square miles of rain forest were destroyed.

The Brazil story is just one of many around the world in which population and environment have crossed swords. The environment has lost, without any real benefit to people.

When asked about 1991's problems, science writer Isaac Asimov told a *USA Today* reporter, "Above everything else are the problems of the environment and population. As long as the population keeps increasing in the world, the environment will continue to deteriorate in every way. And life will become harder and more miserable for all of us."

The major problems concerning the environment and population involve pollution of the air, degradation of the land, and poisoning of the water sources. Another very important problem is the imbalance between nations that have been industrialized for a long time and those that are just beginning to find ways to support their people.

## The Air

The more people there are, the more industry there is, and the more cars there are on the roads. All of this adds up to more chemicals polluting the air.

Fossil fuels are used primarily to make electricity, to transport people and products, and to carry on industrial processes. And the burning of fossil fuels—particularly in cars and electric-power production—is the major source of air pollution around the world.

Some of the pollutants are visible. They consist of tiny partially burned particles that spew out of smokestacks and car exhausts. When air pollution is really bad, people choke and gasp. In Mexico City, soon to be the most populated city on Earth, it's usually not even safe for children and old people to go outdoors because of the chemicals in the air.

Other pollutants are gases. Ozone, for example, is a form of oxygen made of three atoms of oxygen. The oxygen we breathe has two. Ozone is formed when sunlight splits apart the atoms in the pollutants emitted from burning fuels. High levels of ozone in the air make it difficult for people to

*Mexico City is often called the most unhealthy city in the world. Because of severe air pollution, the air is unfit to breathe many days each year.*

*By 2000, São Paulo, Brazil, could be the world's second largest city with a population of 24 million. Supplying adequate housing and jobs while maintaining a healthy environment will be a monumental challenge.*

breathe. Also, ozone is moving beyond the cities into the countryside, where it harms trees and crops.

Other chemicals in the air are transformed into acids and carried long distances on the wind. When these acids drop back to the ground, they harm forests, lakes, and soil.

These are all forms of air pollution that primarily affect individuals and perhaps small areas of the Earth. Certainly they add to the costs that developing countries must face.

However, there is another pollution problem that is affecting the entire planet, a problem that will probably get worse as the Earth's population grows.

**Global Warming.** When fuels are burned, a normal product of the combustion, or burning, process is the gas called carbon dioxide ($CO_2$). Plants absorb carbon dioxide and use it in the presence of sunlight to make sugars, which they burn for energy. The plants then give off oxygen, which animals breathe in. This nicely balanced system has kept life on Earth going for millions of years.

In recent years, however, two things have affected the amount of carbon dioxide in the atmosphere. First, the amount of fuel being burned for energy by developed nations has risen so much that there is more carbon dioxide in the atmosphere than there used to be. At the same time, the deforestation going on all over the world has reduced the number of trees and shrubs that absorb carbon dioxide.

The atmosphere isn't responsible just for the air we breathe but also for the heat that keeps us warm. Sunlight strikes the planet and certain rays are absorbed by the ground. When they are re-emitted as heat (or infrared) rays, those new rays would simply go off into space—if it weren't for the atmosphere.

Because the atmosphere has certain gases with three or more molecules in them (such as $CO_2$), something wonderful happens. The three-atom molecules have the ability to trap heat rays, holding the heat in the atmosphere. This effect has been called the greenhouse effect because the atmosphere traps heat rather like a greenhouse does.

During the last hundred years, humans have been putting extra three-atom molecules into the atmosphere. They are primarily $CO_2$ and other gases given off when fossil fuels—oil, coal, and natural gas—are burned. More heat is being trapped, and most scientists think the Earth is gradually getting warmer, a process called global warming.

No one knows for sure just what will happen if this increase continues. Global warming will change everything

*Deforestation—the clearing of forests—is increasing in many developing countries. This forest in Guatemala is being destroyed by the slash-and-burn method.*

we know about the Earth and its ability to support large populations. The water cycle will work more rapidly, but may not dump its water in the same places. Land that is rich and fertile, such as the middle of North America, may lose the regular water supplies and the seasonal variations that make it such a good place to grow crops. Also, habitats would change as trees and other plants tried to migrate northward to get away from the increasing heat.

As the atmosphere warms, so too would the sea. When water gets warmer, it expands. That expansion would raise sea levels all over the world. Coastal areas and many islands would be flooded. About half the world's population lives within 60 miles (97 kilometers) of the ocean. Many people would lose their homes. They would move to areas that are probably already crowded. And there would be less land for crops all over the world.

Global warming stems from some people wanting too much and from other people having too little. The first group—in the industrialized countries—burn fossil fuels to heat homes, make electricity, produce consumer goods, and move cars and trucks. The second group—in the underdeveloped nations—have destroyed their forests hoping to improve their lives. But now the trees are not there to absorb

*If global warming continues, many coastal areas will be destroyed by flooding and by erosion from rising sea levels.*

*Japan has built a rich economy on exporting consumer goods. The Japanese are now turning to developing countries for new markets.*

carbon dioxide, and so global warming gets worse.

Communications are improving daily around the world. Satellites send television and radio programs to people in developing countries. They know how well most people in developed countries live, and they want their share of the good life. They want the consumer goods that we enjoy. They want electricity and refrigeration. Their governments are doing what they can to improve the lives of their people.

## Global Impact of Population

Paul Ehrlich devised an equation that shows the impact of population on the environment:

*Impact per person*
X *Number of persons*
*Total Environmental Impact*.

If the impact or the number of persons increases, the total impact increases.

In North America and Europe, each person makes a large impact on the environment by buying so many things, using so much energy, and by driving so much. We make as great an impact on the environment as much larger populations

*Living in southern California means driving a car on crowded freeways. Many people commute four to five hours daily, wasting valuable fossil fuel and contributing to air pollution.*

that consume very little. If a large nation starts to consume more, as developing nations are likely to do, then the Total Environmental Impact could become overwhelming.

Americans already put three-quarters of the excess carbon dioxide into the atmosphere. Imagine what would happen to the Total Environmental Impact if all nations burned as much fossil fuel as we do.

Between 1950 and 1985, the amount of carbon dioxide emitted by power plants and deforestation and other human sources increased by 3.1 percent. However, during that same period, the population of the world increased only 1.9 percent. Thus increased technology, primarily in the developed, wealthier countries, accounted for an increase of 1.2 percent.

What does all this mean? It means that almost two-thirds of the increased carbon dioxide in the atmosphere was there because so many more people were using fossil fuels. If the population of the world continues to grow at such a rate, it will be nearly impossible to stop global warming. By 2025, the Third World countries will be putting as much $CO_2$ into the atmosphere as the whole world did in 1990.

What happens if global warming is not slowed? Most scientists think that there could be major disasters on our planet, especially as population increases.

In Bangladesh, for example, much of the land would be covered by the sea. The country already has major problems because of both its low-lying location and its huge population, which could reach 324 million people in the next hundred years. Many of those people would become refugees, forced out of their homes and into whatever lands would take them.

If even a "mere" 1 percent of the world's people were turned into refugees by global warming by the year 2020, there would be 80 million homeless people! They will need to be fed. They will need to be housed.

Nations already in trouble with their resources because of global warming are not going to welcome refugees. It's certainly possible that the refugees, unable to find what they need, might take it—starting a whole new series of wars.

*This refugee camp in Malaysia was home to 36,000 Vietnamese. If global warming continues and people are unable to live where they always have, how many refugees can the nations of the world accommodate?*

## Forests, Water, and Soil

Forests, water, and soil are closely intertwined—as is everything in the environment. The roots of trees hold water in the soil. When the trees are gone, the soil dries and begins to erode. It is washed into lakes and rivers by rain; it is carried away on the wind. Experts estimate that 24 billion tons (21.6 billion metric tons) of fertile topsoil disappear every year.

As population increases, these three vital parts of Earth will continue to break apart, or degrade.

**Deforestation.** The story of what has been happening in Brazil is just one reason for deforestation. Forests the world over are being cut down at an incredible rate. Amazonian businessmen cut down forests for mahogany. Indonesians cut them for teak and rattan. These woods are popular in American and European furniture. But more than half of the destruction of forests takes place for a very simple and basic reason: people need fuel.

For large numbers of people in developing countries, the woods around them are their only source of fuel. And as the population of a village expands, the women and children have to go farther and farther to find wood. It is estimated that two-thirds of the deforestation worldwide has been due to increased population.

Close to 3 billion people may soon be living in areas where there isn't enough wood left to use as fuel. In Ethiopia, which once was covered by green forests, only 4 percent of the land is still covered with trees today.

The more people there are, the more wood is gathered, the more land is cleared, the more soil is eroded. When tree roots are gone, the water from rains and floods runs quickly over the top of the soil and out into the ocean or lakes. It is expected that by the year 2000, an area of the world totaling one and a half times the size of the United States will have turned to desert—without moisture, without topsoil.

**Water.** More than 70 percent of the water withdrawn from the Earth by people is used for crops. But less than half of that water actually reaches the growing plants. The rest is wasted, especially by watering systems that send water arcing into the air where it evaporates before it hits the ground.

When water is pumped from the ground faster than rainfall can replenish it, the water table gets lower and lower. In China, the capital city of Beijing is already losing 3 feet (0.9 meter) or more of groundwater each year. The ground may sink along with the water table, cracking buildings and destroying fields. But also, it then costs a lot more to pump water out of the ground. Wells run dry. The cost of water rises. The cost of food rises. More people go hungry.

*The deserts of northern Africa are slowly growing larger and threatening nations in central Africa. When forests such as this one in Ghana are destroyed, the topsoil erodes and the land becomes useless. Many developing nations are now working on projects to restore the forests.*

**The Loss of Good Land.** Land is not just the ground beneath our feet. It is one of the most important resources on our planet. Without land, air, and water, nothing could survive. Without good land, bearing nutrient-filled topsoil, nothing could grow.

When the number of people in an area increases, a

certain amount of land is needed to support them. They need land to live on. Industries, schools, and stores require additional land. And more farmland is needed to grow crops to feed them. However, the first two take available land from the third.

**Every day, another 1,600 people are added to California's population. That means another 240 acres (96 hectares) of land are covered with buildings or concrete for roads and parking lots—land that might otherwise have been used for agriculture. Across the United States, as much as 10 percent of all farmland has been lost in recent years through erosion or urban construction.**

For every person added to the world's population, an additional 6,450 square feet (600 square meters) of land is taken up by factories, roads, and homes. It is usually good agricultural land that is taken out of production because towns aren't built in deserts and jungles.

People often ask, "Well, why don't developing countries just clear more land for agriculture?" That seems reasonable at first, but if the land does not have enough natural water to support a crop, it will have to be irrigated. There are many places on the Earth where there is no longer enough water available for irrigation. And irrigation costs money. In addi-

*Water projects such as this dam in Iran* (left) *have made unproductive land useful through irrigation. But irrigation can also cause land to become useless. These farmworkers on a Jamaican sugar plantation* (right) *are working to desalinate land made salty through years of irrigation.*

tion, irrigation projects such as building dams to form reservoirs are now known to damage factors in our environment beyond the land that is flooded by the reservoir.

If the land does not drain well, the water accumulates in the soil until it drives oxygen out. Plant roots cannot thrive in such waterlogged soil. Croplands around the world have been irrigated so long that more land becomes too degraded to use each year.

At the opposite extreme are the places where the climate is dry and water evaporates very quickly when it is spread over the land. Even fresh water has some salt in it—though usually less than 1 percent the salt in ocean water. When water evaporates instead of running into a river, it leaves salt behind. Year after year, those salts accumulate until the land becomes useless. This process is called salinization.

Land can also be poisoned by pesticides. A great deal more pesticide is sprayed on plants than ever actually hits pests. Much of the pesticide soaks into the soil, gradually accumulating and poisoning it. The rest runs off the land

and poisons the water sources.

There is a particularly sad note about pesticides. A number of them, such as DDT, have been outlawed by the United States government as too dangerous to use. And yet the companies that make them continue to sell them in other countries around the world. They are just as dangerous there, and some products that come back into the United States have been poisoned by those pesticides. A law that would outlaw this "circle of poisons" has been introduced into Congress.

The United Nations projects that by the end of the twenty-first century, the population of developing countries should stabilize at about 10 billion—almost twice what it is today. Each of those additional 5 billion people will take up about 6,000 square feet (558 square meters) in new paving and housing. That amounts to 690 million acres (280 million hectares), which is equal to almost one-third of Canada. Much of this land will come from existing farmland. That farmland will have to be replaced, and a lot more put into production in order to feed all those people. Most of that new farmland will come from existing forests. Again, global warming will get worse.

## The People with the Most . . . and the Least

The Third World countries know that Earth's future is not just their problem. In March 1991, representatives of 34 developing countries met in Mexico City and spoke out publicly for the first time. They blamed the industrialized nations for the state of the planet. They said that the Third World did not create the pollution problems so it was up to the nations that created them to clean them up.

Alan Durning of Worldwatch Institute says, "The world's 1 billion meat eaters, car drivers, and throwaway consumers are responsible for the lion's share of the damage that humans have caused to common global resources." There are about 4.3 billion other people on the planet, people who have to make do with the tiny portion of the resources left over after the industrialized nations use most of them. The industrialized nations also contribute the most to environmental degradation the world over.

The average person in a developing country uses most of the energy sources available for the basic business of feeding himself and his family. In the United States, however, the average person uses 100 times more energy for maintaining a convenient lifestyle than he or she uses for the growing, processing, or distributing food. In the United States, fossil-fuel use has risen 60 percent since 1950. It goes mainly for making electricity and running cars.

*A crowded street in Bangladesh looks nothing like a California freeway. People in developing nations use less fossil fuel and contribute less to environmental problems than people in developed nations.*

*Disposing of municipal waste is a worldwide problem. Landfills in industrialized countries are running out of space (left). In the impoverished black homelands of South Africa, waste is often not picked up at all (right). Rural migrants are moving into urban areas too fast for city services to keep pace with the growth.*

**FACT**

**According to Zero Population Growth, one American uses the same amount of energy as 3 Japanese, 6 Mexicans, 14 Chinese, 38 Indians, 168 Bangladeshis, or 531 Ethiopians. The poorest 20 percent of the world's people use only 4 percent of its resources. The richest 20 percent use 58 percent.**

Our resources on the planet, such as water and land, can handle some degree of pollution. Natural systems have the ability to cleanse themselves, but only to a certain extent. Humans have added more pollutants to the environment than natural recycling can handle. If the planet is to have a future that includes life as we know it, growth in developing countries is going to have to happen in ways that keep the environment in balance. For example, developed countries may have to give up the use of coal so that developing countries, which can't afford nuclear power, can burn coal without additional harm to the atmosphere. (Of course, that means that we must develop ways of producing nuclear power that do not endanger the environment and people's lives—not an easy task.)

**Movement to Cities.** About 1960 the movement of unemployed people from rural areas to cities began in Third World countries. They were looking for relief from poverty, which seemed very bad in the country. But most of the urban migrants found only more poverty.

If they are lucky, a family of five or six may find one room to live in. Families in twenty such rooms may share one bathroom, which works only part of the time—if it works at all. However, they might end up like the boy at the beginning of this chapter, living in cardboard boxes covered with aluminum or plastic scrap. They have no toilet and no running water. Such slums or shantytowns smell bad, breed disease and vermin, and destroy hope.

If the movement to cities—called urbanization—continues while the population also increases, the big cities of the world will double in population faster than the developing countries as a whole. City populations in Africa are expected to increase by about 540 percent between 1985 and 2025. Towns are growing 5 percent a year—$2^1/_2$ times faster than country areas. There is no time or money to build the roads, housing, utilities, and services that they require.

Oddly enough, while the plight of cities gets worse, such urbanization may actually have a positive influence on population growth. People living in cities tend to have fewer children than people in rural areas. So, as more people move to cities, population growth may slow. But in the meantime, cities are getting very crowded.

## How Are Things Going to Get Fixed?

Three main factors hurt the planet's environment: overuse of the world's resources by the wealthy nations; the technology that uses the resources and produces considerable waste in the process; and a huge population. Many people think that if we can reduce any of those three factors, the environmental degradation will improve.

Leaders of developing countries know that if they are going to have a future, they must pay attention to the environment as they build. But it's not going to be easy. It takes more money to build businesses that are environmentally sound than it does to modernize without paying attention to the environment (as industrial nations have done until recently). And cash is a problem for all those nations.

**FACT**

**Developing countries—mostly in the Southern Hemisphere—currently owe about $1 trillion to developed countries—mostly in the Northern Hemisphere. They pay about $30 billion each year in interest alone, so they have limited funds for their own industrial development.**

We have a circular problem. If we want to reduce the population so that the environment is not degraded further, we must increase the standard of living. People with higher standards of living tend to have fewer babies. To increase the standard of living, we need to have industrial development and modernization in Third World countries. Increasing the industrial development will, according to today's standards, increase the damage to the environment.

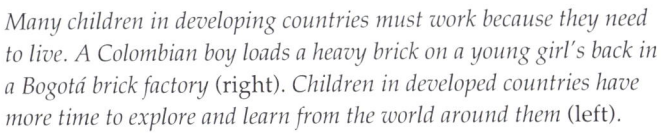

*Many children in developing countries must work because they need to live. A Colombian boy loads a heavy brick on a young girl's back in a Bogotá brick factory* (right). *Children in developed countries have more time to explore and learn from the world around them* (left).

When large numbers of people have to work and find food, countries are apt to take the short-term answer to problems instead of the long-term, and who can blame them? But short-term answers call for cutting down forests, exporting valuable raw materials, and letting soil erode.

The developing countries certainly don't want to harm the environment. The South Commission is a group of people representing the nations and continents in the Southern Hemisphere—an area with fewer resources and more people. The commission was formed in 1987, with Dr. Julius Nyerere, the president of Tanzania, as chairman.

The commission's report, *The Challenge to the South,* said: "In the long run the problem of overpopulation of the countries of the South can be fully resolved only through their development. But action to contain the rise of population cannot be postponed. The present trends in population, if not moderated, have frightening implications for the ability of the South to meet the twin challenges of development and environmental security in the twenty-first century."

# Chapter 5

# Family Planning

A WOMAN CARRIES A VERY heavy burden in many developing countries. She has as many children as possible so that some will survive to grow up and support the parents. While she is bearing and raising the children, she needs to do much of the work on the family's subsistence-level farm. She plants, hoes, harvests, and tends livestock. She and the children collect water each day. In addition, three or four times a week she gathers wood for cooking. That could involve walking several miles, chopping down thick branches (if she is lucky enough to find them), and carrying the load back over those same long miles—and all in hot, humid weather. It is probable that during her younger years she will do all this work with one child at her side, another on her back, and a third not yet born.

How could that woman's life have been improved? Certainly by having more income. But probably also by producing fewer children. In many parts of the world, the two problems are interrelated.

Developing countries are the same way—they need more income, and they would thrive better if their citizens produced fewer children. Many countries are trying to do something about both interrelated situations.

There is a constant debate about how to limit population. Most people think that we can reduce population growth primarily by putting more effort into family-planning programs, which teach women and men how to limit their family's size. Others think that economic development—higher income—is more important.

*This mother in the African nation of Burkino Faso is like many mothers in developing nations. To help support her family, she must work in the fields all day while caring for her young child.*

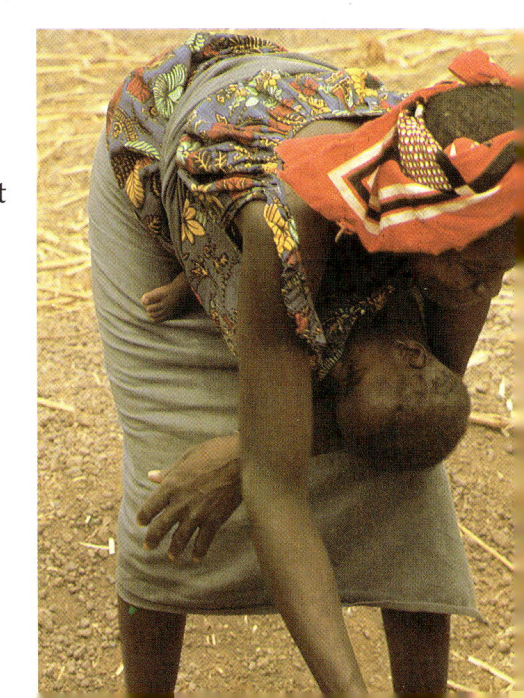

*Many women in developing countries have very few choices. They are expected to marry, have large families, and work long hours while raising their children. This Nepalese woman herds the family's goats and sheep to market with her child on her back.*

There has to be a chance for that woman and her husband to increase their family income.

However, economic development may not be possible unless the population is kept down. Otherwise, whatever growth there is, will be spread out over more and more people. The International Conference on Population, which was held in Mexico City in 1984, agreed that family planning and economic development have to work together for either to succeed.

The United Nations holds that five factors determine the size of a family: the status of women in society, health care available to mothers and children, availability of family planning, family income, and education for all.

## Taking Control

When a survey of women around the world was made by the United Nations, about 500 million women who already had families said that they did not want more children. Most of them, however, have neither the knowledge nor the means to do anything about it.

Men and women who have sexual intercourse run the

risk of becoming pregnant. In fact, 85 percent of all couples who have sexual intercourse without using some means of birth control become pregnant within a year. Wishing won't make it otherwise, either in the forests of Indonesia or the cities of North America.

Because sex is a normal, healthy part of the lives of men and women, the possibility of pregnancy is always present. The consequences—babies—have an effect on the whole society.

But family planning means more than just limiting the number of babies a family has. It is part of a total environment of change that gives women freedom they have never had before—freedom to make their own choices about how they are going to live.

Population control is not family planning. Family planning is a personal decision to use the birth-control methods available. Population control, on the other hand, is a political issue. The government has to plan the use of resources. It might impose extra taxes on families with more children. Whatever the government decides about population control,

*The lifeline of many developing countries is the export of raw materials to developed nations. The lifeline of these Andean Indian women is the money received from working in this Bolivian zinc mine—often with a child tied to her back.*

75

it can happen only through family planning.

In the past, population growth slowed because of external factors, such as a plague, famine, or war. This is the first time in history that the growth rate can go down because individuals can make the choice to have fewer children than their parents and grandparents had—and have the means of carrying out that choice.

## Preventing the Conception of a Child

Birth control is any method, medicine, or device used to prevent conception, the joining of a woman's egg and a man's sperm. Throughout most of history, the main means of such *contra*ception has been to refrain from sexual intercourse. This is still the best (and only guaranteed) way, but it isn't always possible, especially for married couples.

The use of birth control is an important part of family planning. Its use allows a couple to have sexual intercourse with a reduced chance of getting pregnant. In industrialized nations, many couples use various methods to delay having their first child. Others decide to have no children at all.

*Family planning instruction is a large part of the regular routine at this hospital in Kenya. Projects such as these are educating women about birth-control methods and family health care.*

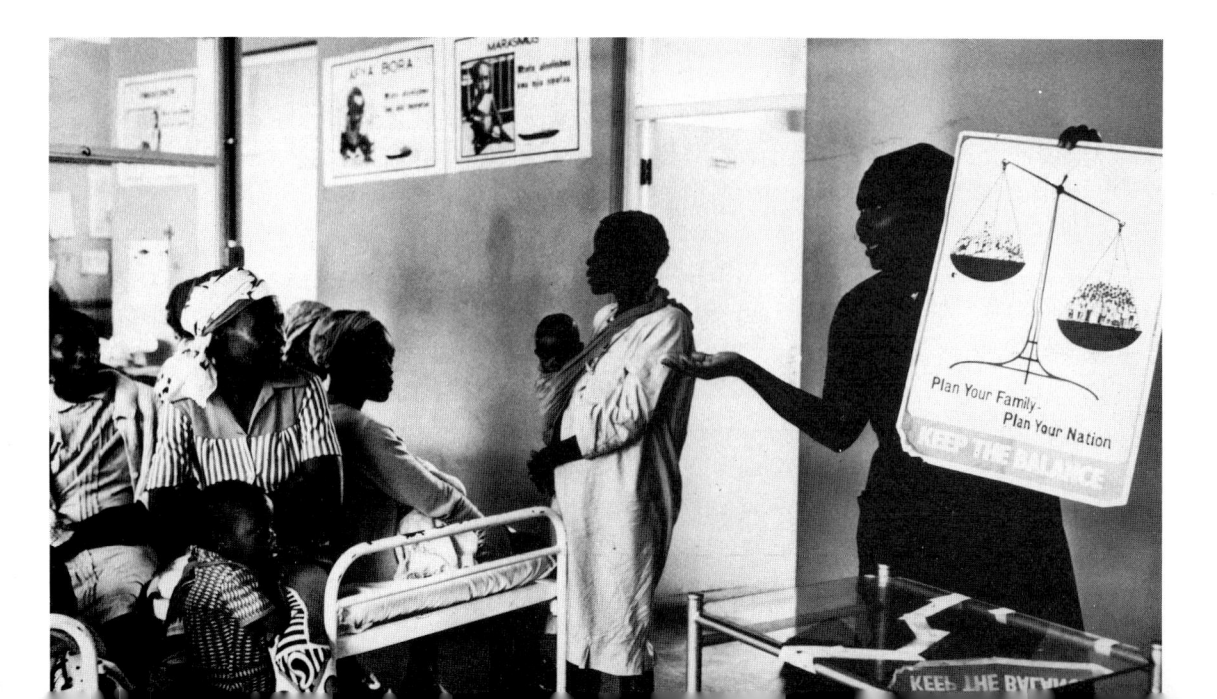

> Zero Population Growth, an international association that is working to achieve a stabilized world population, says that one out of every seven married couples in the United States makes a thought-out choice not to have children.
>
> **FACT**

Since scientists learned how the human body works, many couples have been able to refrain from intercourse during the time when a woman is most likely to get pregnant—eight days during the middle of the interval between her menstrual periods. But, people aren't perfect, and this method, one of a variety called the rhythm method, often fails because people aren't always exact, and other factors can affect the timing.

Rhythm is also called fertility awareness because it involves an awareness of a woman's ovulation cycle. It is usually the only method used by many people who oppose contraception on religious or moral grounds. It is the only contraceptive method approved for members of the Roman Catholic Church, for example.

**Contraceptives.** Contraceptives are medicines or devices that prevent conception. Different contraceptive methods have been passed down over the generations, but until recently they were not very reliable.

One of the oldest devices is the condom. This is a rubber sleeve that unrolls to cover a man's penis, thus preventing sperm from entering the woman's uterus. A condom is discarded after intercourse. A new one must be used each time. Condoms are popular again because their use helps limit the chances of passing sexually transmitted diseases such as AIDS between sexual partners. Unfortunately, condoms tend to deteriorate in tropical climates.

Since the 1950s, various hormone medicines have been available that control the release of eggs (ovulation) in the female. Often referred to as "the Pill," such medicines are available by prescription in most countries. In developing countries, they are too expensive for many women to buy.

Norplant is a capsule that can be inserted in a tiny cut in a woman's upper arm. For five years it delivers a continuous supply of a very tiny amount of chemicals that prevent ovulation. Then the capsule has to be replaced. China and Indonesia are two populous countries that have approved Norplant for use in family planning. A newer hormone implant called Capronar is expected to be widely used in developing countries.

Devices used by women that are similar to a condom are the diaphragm and cervical cap. These are flexible rubber devices that fit inside the woman's body, closing off the cervix—the entrance to the uterus. In developing countries, these devices may cause infections because they have to be washed regularly in clean water, which is often not available. Similar disposable devices called contraceptive

*The government of Indonesia supports family planning programs. This health care worker explains the different forms of birth-control methods available to a client.*

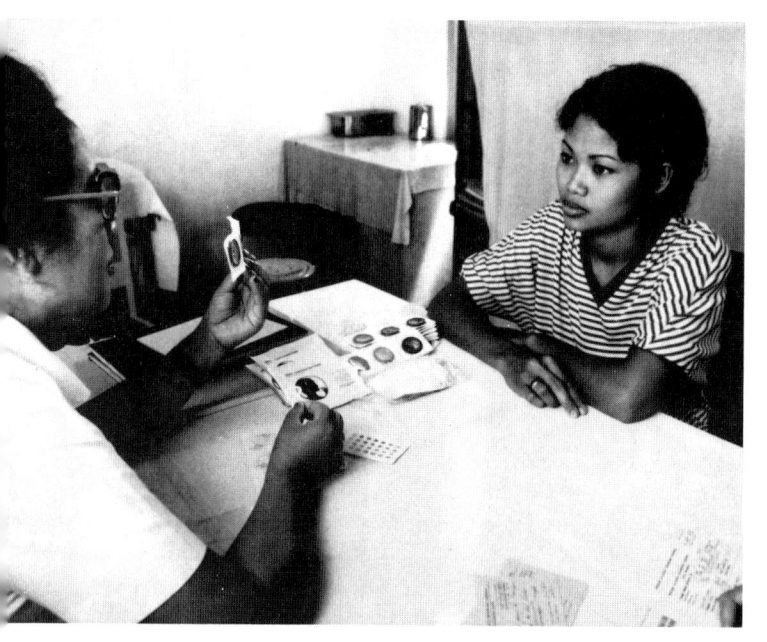

*Family planning posters are used to remind the people of Kenya that having children means providing good, responsible care for each child.*

sponges are also fairly expensive and are not often used in developing countries.

Another device is the IUD, or intra-uterine device. It is a special piece of plastic or copper that is inserted into the woman's uterus and left there for a year or more at a time. It prevents pregnancy by chemically interfering with conception. IUDs are the most popular kind of contraceptive in the world. It is estimated that almost 100 million women worldwide have used IUDs.

The United Nations Population Fund reports that a newer contraceptive is expected to be very helpful in developing countries. The vaginal ring, developed by the World Health Organization, is worn internally, where, over a period of several months, it gradually releases hormones that prevent conception.

**Permanent Contraception.** Contraceptives are usually regarded as temporary. A woman can stop taking the Pill when she wants to get pregnant. A couple can decide not to put on the man's condom. A more permanent procedure that prevents conception is called sterilization. A man can be sterilized by having a quick surgical procedure called a vasectomy. In a vasectomy, a tube called the vas deferens is cut. This tube runs from the sperm-making testicles to the prostate gland where sperm is stored. When the vas deferens is cut, sperm cannot be ejected.

According to Zero Population Growth, about 10 percent of all American men had vasectomies by 1990, and about 400,000 more are performed in the United States each year.

A woman can be sterilized by having her Fallopian tubes tied. These tubes connect the ovaries, where the eggs are stored, to the uterus. The procedure is called a tubal ligation. In the United States, Canada, and Europe, many women choose to have their "tubes tied" after the birth of a second or third child.

If a man decides that he wants to have children after all, he may try to get the vasectomy reversed. However, in a newer procedure, a small amount of liquid plastic is injected into the vas deferens. It forms a plug that keeps sperm from getting through. Then, if the man later wants the procedure reversed, the plug can simply be removed. A woman's tubal ligation, on the other hand, cannot be reversed.

It has been estimated that making family planning available to everyone in the world will require the spending of between $8 billion and $10 billion each year. But there is no really good means of contraception available in developing countries. Diaphragms have to be washed in clean water. Pills are expensive. Condoms, while easy and effective to use, are thought by some men to reduce pleasure and to be a hassle to put on. So sterilization has become the way of choice of limiting families in much of the world.

Work is being done on other procedures and chemicals,

especially an anti-pregnancy vaccine that can be reversed when a couple chooses. However, few American companies are involved in researching such a vaccine because one company produced an IUD that turned out to be very harmful. The company failed to remove the IUD from the market and is being sued by many people.

## Abortion

An *abortion* is the deliberate stopping of a pregnancy. (A *miscarriage* is the accidental stopping of a pregnancy.) Doctors and other trained people around the world perform abortions under various circumstances. In China, for example, it takes only a decision on the woman's part that she doesn't want to have the baby.

An abortion consists of having the embryo (the developing fertilized egg) removed from the woman's uterus—sometimes by scraping it out, and sometimes by suctioning it. The procedure should usually be done only within the first three or four months of pregnancy.

*Family size in industrialized countries is usually smaller than family size in developing countries. The average Japanese family with one or two children has a higher standard of living than large families in less developed countries.*

A more controversial method has been developed, technically known as RU-486, but called the "abortion pill." It is taken by a woman after sexual intercourse and works by causing her to menstruate, which flushes the fertilized egg out of her uterus.

Produced in France, the abortion pill became available in 1988. The manufacturer removed it from the market when many people opposed to abortion objected to it. However, the French government demanded that it be made available in the interests of public health. In 1991, Great Britain became the second country to approve its use.

**The American Situation.** During most of U.S. history, abortions were against the law. When teenage girls got pregnant by accident, or women decided that they did not have the energy to raise another child, they often tried to find a person (preferably a doctor, of course) who would perform an abortion. But because abortion was illegal, the procedure could not be done in a hospital. Many women were sterilized and many others died because of the dirty conditions under which these illegal abortions were performed. These are often called "back alley" abortions.

In 1973 the U.S. Supreme Court ruled in a case called *Roe vs. Wade* that according to the Constitution, a woman has the right to make her own decisions about her body, thus freeing women to have abortions if they wanted. However, in 1990, the Supreme Court decided that abortion was not a constitutional matter and that each state could make its own laws.

At least 20 states are working on laws that require a teenager to get permission of one or both parents or a judge before having an abortion. Although the rate of teenage

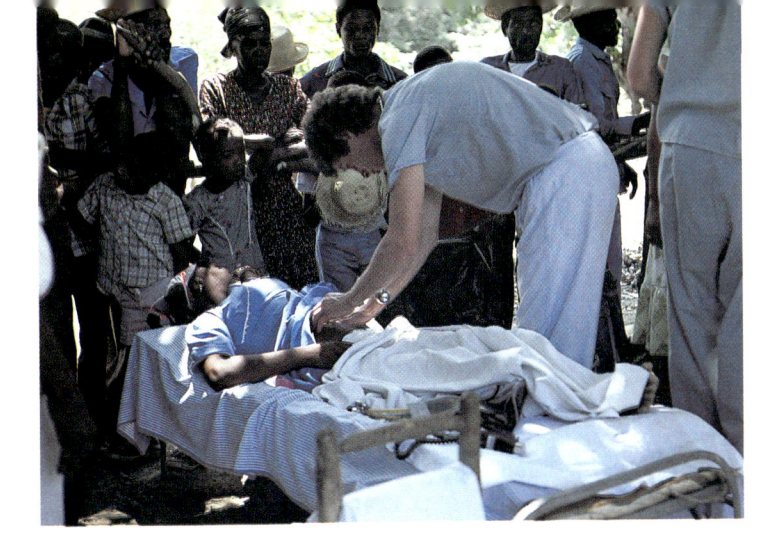

Having children means a lifetime of responsibility. Receiving adequate health care before a baby's birth is important. This mother in Haiti (above) is being checked by a doctor who travels to rural areas. Caring for children properly is a concern when mothers have to work. Women in China (right) and Mexico (top right) take children to work—one to rice paddies and the other to a vendor's stall on the streets of Mexico City where she packs her child in a box The number of teenage mothers in the United States (bottom right) is growing. Trying to juggle school and child care is a difficult task. Many women in the United States are single heads of families totally responsible for their children (below). They often live in low-income areas, full of crime and pollution.

pregnancy in the United States is high, about 75 percent of all abortions performed in America are done on women over the age of 20.

Many people hope that the Supreme Court will reinforce its earlier position and once again declare abortions legal under all circumstances. They want women to have the freedom of choice. Other people hope that the court will outlaw abortion completely.

**FACT**

**Each year, more than 1 million American teenagers become pregnant, while they themselves are still basically children. That is twice the rate of teenage pregnancies in Canada. Less than one-third of the pregnant teenagers are married. About half of these pregnancies result in a live birth. The others end in abortion or miscarriage. Less than half of the teenagers who become mothers at age 17 or younger will ever complete their high school education.**

**Controversy about Abortion.** Abortion is always controversial because many people regard it as morally wrong to stop the development of a growing embryo or fetus. (An unborn baby is called a fetus after the first three months.) They insist that an embryo is a human being with full human rights from the moment of conception.

About 53 countries around the world, where about 25 percent of the Earth's people live, outlaw abortion. However, according to the World Health Organization, as many as 200,000 women in those countries die each year from badly done illegal abortions.

Other people feel that until the unborn child could survive if it were born (at least six months), abortion is not wrong. They especially feel that grown women and their husbands have the right to decide whether to give birth or not.

## Arguments Against Family Planning

If people have access to family-planning information and contraceptives, why doesn't everyone use them? There are many reasons—some religious, some moral, and some cultural.

In many nations of the world, men have traditionally taken pride in having large families. *Time* magazine reported that there is a man in Kenya who brags that he has fathered 497 children.

In many developing countries, an important part of education for family planning, therefore, is to encourage men to change their attitudes. Health-care workers are showing them that everyone can be healthier, that there will be more money available within the family with fewer children, and that small families do not mean the men are less masculine.

*Developing nations such as India are focusing some of their resources to educate men about their responsibility for family planning.*

*In most Muslim countries, women don't have many choices and are expected to have large families. Both the total fertility rate and the infant mortality rate are high in the least developed countries, of which many are Muslim.*

**The Religious View.** A number of religious groups are opposed to family planning. They feel that the number of children a woman has is up to God and that people should not interfere in God's decision. Many conservative Christians think that family planning is wrong. The Roman Catholic Church is officially opposed to contraception by any means except the rhythm method. In 1968, the pope, the international head of the Catholic church, reconfirmed the Catholic church's position.

Official religious positions, however, don't necessarily stop family planning. Italy, which is the home of the Vatican, headquarters of the Roman Catholic Church, has the lowest birth rate in the world—only 1.3 children per couple. In Quebec, Canada, where the people are predominantly Catholic, the birth rate is lower than in the rest of Canada. In fact, the Quebec government has offered cash bonuses to people who produce extra children because they feel that the population needs to be built up again. In the United States, some Catholics feel that the decision to have more children should be in their own hands, not their church's.

Muslims (people who believe in the religion of Islam) make up almost 20 percent of the world's population. Unlike the Catholic church, this religion has no central leader and no solid opinion against contraception. And yet Muslims lead the world in high birth rates. And, Muslims are concentrated in the poorest countries, which have the highest infant mortality rates in the world—about 150 babies die out of every 1,000 born.

Progress is being made, however. In 1991, the conservative Muslim country of Iran made sterilization legal. The government even offered free procedures to any man or woman who wanted one. However, women must already have three children and must have their husbands' permission. Before 1991, the average Iranian woman had produced 6.3 living children.

In Indonesia, religious leaders were included in government discussions about the country's population problems. Instead of opposing family planning, they now back it.

## Bringing Family Planning to the People

In most developing nations where family planning has been introduced it is part of a general program to improve the health of the people. Nurses, doctors, and midwives (women who have been trained especially in caring for pregnant women and delivering babies) are sent out into the villages, usually on a regular schedule. As one health-care worker helps a man who has cut his leg, another might be

*As part of an overall rural development program, Panama's government is improving health care for some rural farm families. Children are vaccinated, and couples are taught about family planning.*

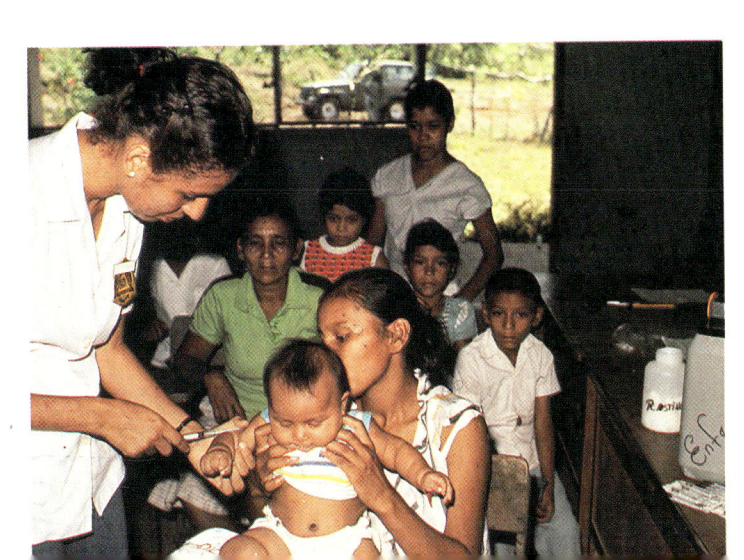

weighing a new baby, and a third could be conducting a class on good nutrition for the family.

In this helpful setting, women are informed that there are ways to keep from getting pregnant. Those women who are in ill health because they've had too many children and those who have trouble carrying a baby for the full nine months are especially told that there is another way, that they don't have to keep having babies.

Because they are often worried about having enough children grow up, the women are also taught about better methods of sanitation, how to wash food, and other actions that limit the spread of disease that might kill children. When they see that more children might live to grow up, they are more willing to use family planning.

In Latin America, a television soap opera called "Polite Society" is used to both entertain and educate the public about family planning. It is reaching more people than counselors going into the villages and shantytowns ever could. In Nigeria, a television variety show has regular skits about family planning. Both of these shows have increased the number of people seeking contraceptives.

## Programs Worldwide

The population of a nation cannot be stabilized until the birth rate is down to approximately 2.1 children per woman. The birth rate could be brought down just by giving women who do not want more children access to contraceptives. World population would level off if 75 percent of the people practiced birth control. That would reduce births by 38 percent and drop the death rate among mothers by 29 percent.

**FACT**

A huge drop in population growth has been achieved in Singapore. In 1965, the average woman in this island republic at the southern tip of Malaysia produced 4.7 babies. The leaders took the threat to society from overpopulation very seriously, and by 1984 the number had dropped to 1.4.

---

The United Nations Population Fund has worked for many years to convince Third World countries that their population growth must be stabilized in order for economic development to take place. During the 1960s and 1970s, the United States supported population work. Many countries, especially those that had been colonies of European nations, feared it was an attempt to kill off peoples of a different color. But, gradually, they began to admit that they had a problem.

Each country has to decide for itself whether and how its population growth should be brought under control. The religions are different, the land resources are different, the histories are different. And most especially, the government and politics are different.

Without family planning, people generally have only three choices. They can produce children they know they can't take care of properly. They can have abortions. Or they can have the child and put it up for adoption. Some unwanted children are aban-

*In many African nations, family planning principles are taught wherever possible. This traveling health worker in Ghana teaches women about birth-control methods in a meeting outside their homes.*

*Waiting in long lines to purchase almost anything is a fact of life in Moscow. This makes life especially difficult for women who must also work outside the home and raise children.*

doned, perhaps to die. This should never happen.

**The Soviet Union.** In the Soviet Union, just after World War II, the government encouraged women to have as many babies as they could to replace the many millions of Soviet citizens who had died during the war. Women who had eight, ten, even twelve children were honored widely.

However, life in the Soviet Union was difficult. A major part of every day was spent standing in line to get food and other necessities of life. It was usually the women who had to wait, in addition to holding down regular jobs. Many women felt that they could not live in such a way and also raise children.

But the Soviet Union was unable to provide a steady supply of reliable contraceptives. In fact, in recent years, condoms were so poorly made that they leaked and failed to do their job. Therefore, women became pregnant and abortion became a regular part of their lives. The average Soviet woman had between five and seven abortions during her child-bearing years. Each year there were more abortions than there were children born.

When the Soviet Union began to open itself to Western influence in the late 1980s, Western family-planning organizations arranged for Western-style condoms to be manufactured in the Soviet Union.

It is estimated that of the 50 million abortions carried out worldwide each year, perhaps 20 to 30 percent of them were done in the Soviet Union. Whether this will change as the Soviet republics become separate nations will be seen.

**China—Population Control at Work.** China already puts a great deal of effort into health care for everyone, reduction of infant mortality, and full educational benefits for women. This background made it easier to start cutting population growth than it might be in a nation where a woman's status is based on the size of her family. The program has reduced the birth rate to about replacement level, but it has not worked in other respects.

The Chinese leaders decided in the 1970s to control population growth. They thought that China should not have more than about 650 million to 750 million people. They decreed that couples should have only two children. Couples who obeyed the ruling got better housing and other benefits.

However, in 1979, a census showed that the population had already reached the 1 billion mark. The government then took the drastic measure of demanding that new families have only one child.

Unfortunately, the central government felt it had no time to change people's attitudes about the number of children. Instead, they forced the program on the people. A couple had to have a license to have a baby. People were fired from

*In order to control its huge population, China has supported massive public programs to convince Chinese couples that having one child is best. Those couples who have more children risk losing their jobs and apartments.*

jobs and even fined for having more than one child.

Many couples had babies in secret and did not get birth certificates. In a study of those "secret" children versus the babies born under license, the licensed babies showed a greater percentage of boys—up to 112 boys per 100 girls.

A Swedish demographer showed that there were 500,000 girls missing each year the plan was in effect. He calculated the girls were missing because only boys were reported. Also, medical tests early in pregnancy can now reveal if a woman is going to have a girl or a boy. If the test showed a girl, many women may have chosen abortion. Or, if a girl was born, she was put out for private adoption.

People worldwide objected to China's not giving people a choice. The laws were relaxed a bit, and the birth rate started to climb again. It is forecast that China will have about 1.6 billion people before the population stabilizes.

---

**FACT**

**In just fifteen years, Thailand succeeded in cutting its growth rate in half—from 3.2 percent to 1.6 percent by 1990. Much of the success came from the work of one man, economist Mechai Viravaidya. He began by giving away condoms wherever he found a crowd.**

---

**India—A Lack-of-Success Story.** India had the first official family-planning program among less developed nations. It started in 1952 but accomplished little. In 1965, when India had about 480 million people, the program was started again. It reduced the birth rate slightly, but the death rate declined at the same time, so no progress was made. By 1975

India had 600 million people.

The government then required that government workers (who make up well over half the working population) be sterilized after the third child. That just made people angry at the whole idea of family planning, however, and the population growth rate of India has continued to climb. In 1990, population had risen above 850 million. At the present rate, India's population may equal that of China within the next forty years. However, some parts of India are having success in cutting their birth rate.

India's infant mortality rate is twice as high as China's, primarily because it has not given the attention to health care and literacy that China has. India has, however, invested in industry, and as that starts to increase the economic resources of the country, demographic transition may play a role.

## Education and the Status of Women

A Chinese poet said in the year 500 B.C., "If you are thinking a year ahead, sow a seed. If you are thinking ten years ahead, plant a tree. If you are thinking one hundred years ahead, educate the people." And that, of course, includes women.

But for much of the world there is no "of course" about it. Women have a much lower status than men. They're just not very important . . . except as the mothers of children, preferably boys.

*India has stressed industrialization at the cost of environmental degradation. The Ganges River, an important water resource, is polluted with tons of raw sewage and industrial waste. But people still bathe in its waters as part of a religious practice.*

*Education is the key to empowering women. In Bangladesh, both the children* (left) *and their mothers* (right) *are being taught to read at the same time.*

Many people think that a woman derives power from having children. She is powerful as long as her husband and her husband's family are pleased with her, which usually means having more and more children.

In many Third World countries, only boys are sent to school. Education is, of course, beneficial in its own right. But it also works in at least three ways to slow population growth. It shows a woman that change is possible and that she needn't have more children than she wants to have. It helps her acquire the health-care information she needs to raise a healthy family. (If more children survive, women don't need to produce so many children.) And it prepares her for work outside the home and farm. Women who work tend to have fewer children, so the birth rate is further reduced. As literate parents have their own families, that percentage will probably continue to rise.

In villages where women have been given control over the number of children they have, they have also acquired authority over other aspects of their lives. Because of this, their viewpoints are often taken into account, resulting in better management of village resources.

Other changes are further raising the status of women. As developing countries move into the "modern" world, women are acquiring the right to own and inherit property. They are voting and taking charge of their world. In many countries, for example, women have come to realize what bad shape the environment is in and they are working to change things. All of these changes are contributing to the recognition by both women and men that they must take responsibility for their own lives and the Earth.

Slowing population growth is not something that happens because the United Nations says it should or a nation's government wants it to. It will happen only because men and women decide that they themselves will have no children or fewer children than their parents did. It is a personal decision that must start the moment a young person begins to think about sex. And it has to be carried through on a personal basis, for the benefit of the individual, the community, the nations, and the Earth.

*One-child families are common in Denmark where the birth rate is the lowest of any Northern European country.*

# Chapter 6

# The Goal: A Sustainable Earth

POPULATION RISES. Trees are cut down. Soil runs with poisons. Wetlands are drained. Chemicals and garbage are dumped into the ocean. The protective ozone layer in the upper atmosphere gets too thin to do its job. The underground water supply shrinks. The number of cars doubles and redoubles. The number of roads multiplies. And still the population rises.

All these events take place every day, and the situation is getting worse instead of better. Where will it end? If major changes aren't made in the way we treat our planet—and soon—Earth will be unable to support us. Disease could kill many. Starvation could kill many more. Wars might break out between the people living in areas that are completely degraded and those that still had some resources left.

Not a pretty picture. Not even an acceptable picture.

The only answer is to change the way we treat our planet to make certain that Earth will still be a healthy place to live in fifty years, or a hundred, or a thousand. Such a planet is called a sustainable planet. It sustains the life on it without deteriorating.

Sustainability has been defined as the ability of the human race "to ensure that it meets the needs of the present without compromising the ability of future generations to meet their own needs."

And how do we do that? Every one of us can take steps to make sure it happens.

It is impossible to separate the three major factors that will play a role in the sustainability of our planet in coming years: environment, population, and development. Most experts anticipate that if we can keep the world's population below 10 billion, it is possible—through cleaning up the environment and working on the industrialization of Third World countries—to achieve a sound, sustainable Earth. If we don't lift many people out of poverty, the population explosion is bound to continue. And if we don't clean up the environment, none of it will do any good anyway.

**An Earth Experience**

## *No Room to Grow*

Locate two plastic boxes measuring about 6 inches (15 centimeters) by 12 inches (30 centimeters) to serve as planters for this experiment. Shoeboxes lined with foil or wooden boxes would also do. The planters should be at least 4 inches (10 centimeters) deep to allow for root growth. This activity may also be done in a small garden plot in your backyard.

Purchase a package of beet seeds in early spring. Fill each planter with rich soil. In planter #1 place 15 seeds 2 inches (5 centimeters) apart. In the second planter place 45 seeds evenly spaced in the same area. Cover all seeds with 1/2 inch (1.5 centimeters) of soil.

Water the planters thoroughly until the soil is moist down to the bottom. Set them in direct sunlight. Add water only when the top of the soil dries out.

Since beets are root vegetables, it will take at least two months before harvest time. During the growing season observe and measure the leaves in both containers. In the fall pull up the plants and measure the width and length of each root. How does overcrowding affect plant production? What does this tell you about a sustainable Earth?

## Building a Sustainable World

A region or habitat—or planet—has a limit to the population of a species that can thrive in it. That limit is called the *carrying capacity* of the region or habitat—the number that it can support year after year without harm to the environment. The carrying capacity of the planet has been exceeded when a species cannot function without using up nonrenewable resources, which, of course, humans do all the time.

However, humans can use technology to change a region's carrying capacity. For example, a lake that supplies drinking water will be degraded in quality fairly quickly if only a few people dump their raw sewage in it. However, if sewage is first treated to remove most of the degrading elements, the lake can support the water needs of many more people for a much longer time.

For a while it seemed as if irrigation was going to help create a sustainable planet. But most irrigation uses more water than necessary. Much of it evaporates or sinks into the ground without getting near the plants. Year after year, we lose more land in the resulting salinization. Clearly, irrigation will not contribute much to a sustainable future.

*Indonesia is trying to protect watershed areas by planting elephant grass as ground cover. Later, trees will be planted in an effort to reforest thousands of acres of valuable land.*

If irrigation isn't the answer, what is? Agricultural scientists have to investigate the crop potential of as many plants as possible, plants that could be grown in the areas where they originated, so that extra watering and fertilizing isn't necessary. Nature did it. We can copy nature, if we will.

When tropical rain forests and other dense, old forests around the world are cut down in one grand sweep, numerous species of plants and animals may become extinct. Most of them probably have never even been identified by biologists. We are losing the genes in those plants that might help produce stronger, more productive species.

Many agriculturists and scientists have become concerned about *gene erosion*—the loss of many varieties of plants through deforestation and Green Revolution farming. More than 100 countries are maintaining *gene banks*, collections of plants and seeds that preserve genetic diversity.

*Using irrigation to grow cotton in the deserts of California makes no sense. Cotton should be grown where the climate is naturally wet and humid.*

## Taking Steps

Anything that caring humans do to protect the Earth and its environment helps in the development of a sustainable planet. There are numerous small steps that can be taken, such as increases in the Debt-for-Nature idea. This program proposes that developing countries, which owe huge amounts of money to Western nations, would agree, for example, not to cut down trees in a certain area in return for cancellation of some of the debt.

*The National Seed Storage Laboratory in Colorado Springs, Colorado, preserves the seeds of many different plant varieties by using liquid nitrogen. The collection includes domestic and foreign species, wild relatives of food crops, and rare and endangered species.*

Another idea is that any industry that pollutes would have to pay huge taxes for that pollution. This would encourage industries—or governments—to find less harmful ways to run their businesses.

It seems odd that helping less developed nations industrialize is a good thing when developed nations degrade our planet. However, lack of development makes for poverty, and poverty—especially among large numbers of people—plays a major role in the degradation of the environment.

The Organization of Economic Cooperation and Development says, "A successful effort to stabilize world population before it reaches 10 billion would make it easier to achieve a decent life for everyone without destroying the fragile natural resource base on which we all depend."

Reducing population alone is not going to help the people in the world's populated countries unless they are also given a chance to achieve that "decent life" both economically and socially. Poverty will fight against population reduction because poor people tend to have more children.

*In Hato El Cedral, Venezuela, the llanos (wetlands) are being preserved. Although cattle are still being raised here, it is done without harming the environment. More money is made from ecotourism now than from cattle production.*

*New York City uses huge amounts of fossil fuel to distribute goods to its population. If developing nations are going to prosper, developed nations must conserve resources and also make their distribution more equal internationally.*

**Changing Our Habits.** Developed nations such as the United States, Canada, Japan, and Germany must face the need to consider environmental factors in everything we do.

Goods must be produced with less energy spent. They must be produced without pollutants, even if the process means higher cost. Farmers must not use fertilizer, pesticides, and extra water to produce their crops. We must all reuse and recycle whatever we can. We have a penalty to pay the Earth for our excesses in the past. If we don't start paying it now, there may not be a sustainable future.

Farmers the world over are beginning to make changes in the way they grow crops and livestock. In 1991, representatives from many organizations signed the Asilomar Declaration for Sustainable Agriculture. In it they said, "Our challenge is to meet human needs without denying our descendants' birthright to the natural inheritance of this planet. We must revere the Earth, sustaining and regenerating both nature and our communities. People are a part of nature, not separate from it."

Leaders all over the world are recognizing that the Earth and its environment must be part of all their calculations. They know that the people in developing nations want what we have, and they are trying to get consumer goods and services by building industry in their countries. Fortunately, most leaders know that they won't be able to just charge ahead and take what they want from the planet. Earth can't handle such development. Government agencies that work

102

*The Chinese people use non-polluting bicycle power to transport goods—often out of necessity. Rapid industrialization, however, is creating a big air and water pollution problem.*

on the industrial development of a country must work hand in hand with those agencies responsible for the environment.

The 1990s will be a major period of the world's nations coming to grips with these problems.

## Putting Our House in Order

In 1992, the United Nations Conference on Environment and Development, called the Earth Summit, will be held in Brazil. Up to 40,000 people will attend to lay plans for creating a sustainable, developed planet and deciding who is going to pay for it.

One official says, "The Earth Summit will be the first real effort to put our house in order. Its results may not be miraculous, but they will begin discussions that will go on into the twenty-first century and beyond."

*Reforestation has to be a major priority in many developing nations. These workers in Vietnam are now replanting trees destroyed by years of war.*

103

A major goal of the Earth Summit will be to convince all nations that as far as the environment is concerned there is no such thing as a national border. Industrial air pollution from the United States falls as acid rain in Canada. Eighteen different nations pour wastes into the Mediterranean Sea, and it will take all eighteen to clean it up. What goes into the sea eventually touches all of us.

Much suspicion will have to be overcome. The developing nations insist that the developed nations pay the major costs of environmentally sound development. But they don't want to make a commitment to work on the environment until the developed countries agree to pay for it. However, the developed countries have already made such payments to the developing nations and seen them used for military purposes. Somehow, trust will have to be established.

Unfortunately, not everyone is in agreement about how important a sustainable planet is. Some people want all they can get first—then they'll worry about the Earth.

The general secretary of the Earth Summit says that he will call for a major change in the way business does its accounting to include the environment, but he also insists that environmental protection must not put limits on a developing nation's efforts to achieve a standard of living like that of the Western nations. We can only hope that by the time all the disagreements are sorted out it won't be too late for our planet.

As nations all over the

*Many African nations waste valuable resources needed for economic development in fighting each other. These children dressed in military fatigues are learning that the way to solve conflict is through war.*

planet develop, the marketplace will become global. To achieve a sustainable planet, all nations must include their resources in determining their wealth. Traditionally, wealth has counted only as property or specific assets that a monetary value could be placed on. But what kind of value do you put on a species of deer, for example, or the purity of the water in an underground aquifer?

A sustainable planet will place higher value on crisp, clear air than on warehouses full of products for sale.

The dream of people who care about sustainability is that humans will be able to give their children an environment that is at least as good as, if not better than, the one they themselves inherited. It will take all of us, working together, to achieve that.

*A sustainable planet will place the highest value on maintaining both the beauty and usefulness of Earth's natural resources.*

# Chapter 7
# Not So! – Opposing Views

"WE CAN'T KEEP SAYING that population growth is a horrible thing. The evidence isn't there," says Dennis Ahlburg of the University of Minnesota's Center for Population Analysis and Policy. Ahlburg and other writers point out that ever since Malthus wrote his essays, people have thought population growth was going to make conditions worse and worse. But at the time Malthus wrote, there were only about 1.3 billion people on the planet. Now there are 5.3 billion. And living conditions are much better for most people than they have ever been.

In the late 1960s, the United Nations projected that by the year 2000 there would be 7.5 billion people on Earth. At that time, Paul Ehrlich wrote that in just a few years, "the world will undergo famines—hundreds of millions of people are going to starve to death."

Instead, there was an abundance of food, so much in some parts of the world that crops were burned. Also, to the surprise of many, the birth rate dropped in many countries, so that by 1990—only ten years away from that awesome date of 2000—the projection was down to 6.1 billion.

---

**In 1926, the Federal Oil Conservation Board said that there was only enough oil left in America to last six years. The use of oil has grown in the last decades, but there is still enough available in America alone to last well into the twenty-first century.**

**FACT**

---

Obviously, it's difficult to make accurate predictions about population growth. Equally obviously, population growth alone does not guarantee people difficult lives.

*Unlike other animals, humans have the ability to see beyond their immediate physical needs and make plans for the future.*

## People—The "Ultimate Resource"

Julian Simon is a professor of business administration at the University of Maryland. What Paul Ehrlich calls the "problems" of the growing population, Simon calls the "miracles." He regards it as a miracle that the Earth is actually supporting 5,300,000,000 people. He holds that population growth actually enhances the economic progress that nations make. The reason, he says, is that humans and their ingenuity are "the ultimate resource."

Writer Ronald Bailey has said that Ehrlich's predictions are based on what he calls the "biological fallacy." That means that Ehrlich and other "doomsayers" think that humans behave like other animal species, when in fact our intelligence takes us beyond the rules that govern animal populations. Unlike animals, which might run out of food in their habitat, humans can expand the area in which they obtain their food, or even switch the foods they eat.

According to Malthus and others, more people should mean more starvation. However, since World War II, the income of each person (*per capita* income) in developing countries has increased faster than in developed countries—even as their populations mushroomed.

And in the years between 1971 and 1986, the planet's population grew 2.2 percent and the food available per person grew 0.58 percent. Fewer people went hungry during those years than they had in previous years. Those were the years of the Green Revolution. As we've seen, the final results of the Green Revolution may not all be positive, but,

Professor Simon says, clever humans will come up with another solution to keep progress going.

There will be as much food as people want because people have the capability of responding to demand. Farmers will work harder, expanding the amount of land they plant. Agricultural researchers will do something to increase crop productivity even further. Land will be improved. Human ingenuity will respond.

"It may even be true," says Simon, "that in the long run additional people actually cause food to be less scarce and less expensive, and cause consumption to increase."

In the past, farmers did not farm all the land they had, primarily because there wasn't a market for all they could grow. Simon thinks that if farmers want to use it, there is plenty of land to convert to agriculture.

Of course, Simon agrees, lots of new children, whether in a family or a society, create short-term problems because there are more mouths to feed, but in the long run, they grow up and become productive, thus increasing the family's (or society's) income.

People who believe in Malthus's ideas predicted that as resources became scarcer, prices would rise, taking them out of the reach of many of the world's people. However, this

*These women in Bangladesh* (below) *are learning how to take care of a vegetable garden that will give their families a balanced diet. In Venezuela better farming technology* (left) *has allowed some farmers to produce beyond their immediate needs.*

has not happened. As technology and imagination have solved the problems of making resources available, prices have continued to fall for most resources.

"The basic ingredient in the process, along with the raw elements, is human knowledge," says Simon. "And we develop knowledge about how to use raw elements for our benefit only in response to our needs." He holds that until we need something, we don't find a way of getting it. As our population increases, our needs will increase, and we will develop solutions to solve the problems.

The city/nation of Hong Kong grew from 700,000 people just after World War II (1939 to 1945) to 5.6 million in 1987. According to most projections about the problems of rapid population growth, Hong Kong should be in severe trouble now. And yet it is one of the most prosperous cities on Earth.

*Hong Kong has become both very populated and very prosperous in recent years.*

Nor does Simon think that vast numbers of people should be regarded as a pollution problem on our planet. In fact, he thinks that pollution will be reduced as the population increases. As income rises, so does pollution, and yet, as income rises, so does the money to pay for preventing or cleaning up pollution.

In the short run, there will always be a crisis regarding the availability of some resource, whether because of a war, a drought, a major population shift due to politics, or whatever. But in the long run, the crises even out, making a smooth progression of resources available for growing populations. Population has always risen, and the ability of people to improve their lot in life has risen, too.

"The ultimate resource is people—" says Simon, "skilled, spirited, and hopeful people who will exert their wills and imaginations for . . . the benefit of us all."

## Using Technology Wrongly

Scientist Barry Commoner has spent a lifetime trying to get people to be concerned about pollution of the environment. However, in his 1990 book *Making Peace with the Planet*, he says that it is probably too late. He holds that human technological capability, which he calls Earth's *technosphere*, is now just as important as the atmosphere (air) and the hydrosphere (water) in determining the condition of the planet. The current condition of the environment is the result of the clash between nature, or the ecosphere, and the human technosphere. And the planet is losing.

Commoner objects to the idea that deliberate population reduction is the only way to save the planet. He thinks Ehrlich's idea that Earth is a closed system, with no new resources coming in, is a mistake. Instead, solar energy is

*Human technology has become as important as any of the natural factors on the Earth in determining the shape of our planet. This factory is polluting air, water, and land.*

always being replenished, and the existing elements on the Earth can be reorganized continuously into new resources, like one grand recycling machine.

He would start fixing things by returning some of the riches that were taken away from the countries that were once colonies of Western nations. He thinks that giving those nations, which are among the poorest in the world, their own money would allow them to voluntarily cut back on population growth.

Probably through the whole of human history, industrial development has occurred as a result of the threat of war. But it is now becoming clear that only by ending both the threat of major war and the degradation of our planet can we be sure that the human species will survive.

Commoner, along with many other writers, points out that the environmental costs of production have never been counted into the cost of products. If they were, we would have fewer products. For example, when the environment was threatened by nuclear power plants, safeguards were built into them, and the costs skyrocketed. No construction of new plants has been started in the United States since 1978. If environmental costs were included in the price of products, we would discover that we can't afford them. Certainly the Earth can't afford them.

One problem Commoner sees is that corporations in Western developed nations are responsible to no one but their stockholders. For the most part, the stockholders want short-term profits and don't question the long-term effects of production on the environment.

Plastic is easier and cheaper to handle than wood, even though the processing of plastic creates toxic pollutants. It's easier to apply chemical pesticides than to change agricultural methods, even though the pesticides damage water supplies and poison people. A small fuel-efficient car can't sell for as much as a big "luxury" car. Corporations often make decisions that benefit stockholders instead of the planet.

One real benefit of a larger population is the increasing chance that great minds will be born—and great minds will solve the problems that arise from the population growth of the world.

Demographers say they can't make very accurate long-term predictions about human populations. People are people—and anything can happen. So we don't know for sure what the Earth's human population will be like 100, 50, or even 25 years from now, though we can make pretty good guesses.

It is most likely that the real situation regarding population growth and the Earth's ability to support it lies somewhere in between the positions of those people who believe that Earth may be beyond repairing and those who think that the human mind can accomplish anything.

As the Population-Environment Balance organization says, "The inescapable fact is that each person unavoidably takes a toll on the environment." People have the intelligence to overcome many problems. But we also have the intelligence to avoid the problems when we know about them in advance—if we will take the necessary actions.

*Warfare has brought about a quest for technological progress. But both warfare and technology have had a bad effect on the environment.*

# Chapter 8

# Taking Action

FRANCES MOORE LAPPÉ WROTE an important book called *Diet for a Small Planet* in 1971. It made many people aware of the need for eating lower on the food chain—for our own health as well as the health of our planet. She said in a later edition: "Mammoth social problems, especially global ones like world hunger and ecological destruction, paralyze us. Their roots seem so deep, their ramifications endless. So we feel powerless. How can *we* do anything?"

Sometimes it seems as if we are indeed helpless regarding the planet, but we can each do something that would be helpful.

## A Sustainable World

If we are to have a sustainable world, each of us has to take responsibility for numerous decisions every day: Shall I walk or drive? Can I leave this errand until tomorrow when I have to go to the mall anyway? Do I really need to turn the air conditioner on this afternoon? Did I remember to turn the lights off in the bathroom? Can I make these pants do for another year or do I need a new pair? Shall I bother to carpool? Shall I carry this soda can home to be sure it gets recycled or shall I just throw it away? Shall I put on a sweater or turn the heat up? Shall I cook steak tonight or a broccoli casserole?

Each such decision—the kind that all of us must make daily—seems insignificant by itself. But they add up.

Take a look at how you live and see if you can figure out its effect on the environment. Could everyone on Earth live as you do and still have a planet that will be productive for the next generation?

## An Earth Experience

## *My Kind of Town*

*You have been elected the designer of a new town called Natureville. Your goal is to design a place that is as environmentally sound as it can possibly be.*

*The land space allotted for the town is 2 square miles or 1,280 acres (512 hectares). Use the following measurements to calculate the space required for each structure, road, or place on your blueprint:*

*144 square inches = 1 square foot = 929 square centimeters*
*9 square feet = 1 square yard = 0.836 square meter*
*4,840 square yards = 1 acre = 0.4 hectare*

*Use a large sheet of poster board to represent your town. Figure the number of square yards that must equal 1 square inch on your ground plan.*

*Decide on the size, number, and location of homes, businesses, industry, school, park, waterworks, sewage-disposal plant, fire station, clinic, library, recycling center, tree-lined parkways, roads, railway, and other parts of a North American town. Cut these out of construction paper in different colors, using the same scale as your blueprint. These pieces can be moved around until you settle on the best plan for your town.*

*Think about housing, transportation, jobs, recreation, pollution problems, and green space. Be sure to save some space on the outskirts of the town for a wetland, a wooded lot, and grassland for wildlife habitats.*

*Finally, can you come up with an approximate population count for your town? How many people can live here without it being overpopulated?*

*Take a good look at your own town or city. How close does it come to the ideal that you created? Is your town overpopulated? If the population of your town suddenly doubled because of famine in the countryside, where would the people live? What facilities in your town would you have to change in order to accommodate all those new people? How could they get jobs? How would the additional pollution be handled? What would you have to do to make your town sustainable?*

## Personal Decisions

During the next twenty years, about 3 billion people—probably including you and your friends—will start raising families. Werner Fornos, president of the Population Institute, wrote, "How well these young people are able to implement the basic human right of having only those children they truly want, can care for and love, will mean the difference between a twenty-first century in which we are headed for a better quality of life or environmental armageddon." (Armageddon is the legendary huge conflict that will destroy the world.)

Only you can decide your own position on population and whether or not to contribute to its growth. Teenagers, among whom the population is increasing rapidly, are just as responsible for making that decision as a married couple.

As a young adult, male or female, you will soon need to make some important decisions, decisions that seem very personal but can affect the world. The conception of a child should not be an "accident." Having a child should be a conscious decision based on understanding what is involved—as an individual, as part of a family, as a citizen of a nation, and as an environmentally aware resident of Earth.

*The teenage years used to be a time of carefree fun. But with the increase in teenage pregnancy, venereal disease, and AIDS cases, the choices young couples make are too important to be made carelessly. Sexual decisions can now be life-threatening.*

If you're a young woman, you need to realize that having a baby does not make you more of a woman or prove to someone that you love him. If you're a young man, you need to know that fathering a baby does not prove anything to anyone—except your own carelessness.

**FACT**

In the United States alone, more than 1 million teenagers become pregnant each year. That is more than twice as many as in Canada and England, three times as many as in Sweden, and seven times as many as in the Netherlands.

## Express Your Opinion

Many things about population growth, the environment, and developing nations are in the hands of public officials. Encourage your parents and their friends to vote for officials who have a record of real action when it comes to the environment and are known for contributing to population-control measures around the world. If they are elected, check on whether they keep their campaign pledges.

**Writing Letters.** In writing a letter in which you express your opinion on controversial issues, you might follow these seven tips:

1. Make your letter one page or less. Cover only one subject in each letter.

2. Introduce yourself and tell why you, personally, are for or against the issue.

3. Be clear and to the point.

4. Be specific on whether you want the person to vote "yes" or "no."

5. Write as an individual. The environmental groups you belong to will have already let the legislator know their stand on the issue.

6. When you get a response, write a follow-up letter to re-emphasize your position and give your reaction to your legislator's comments.

7. Write again to thank your legislators if they vote the way you asked them to.

On issues concerning state legislation or to express your opinion about laws up for action by your state or provincial government, check at the library for the name and address of one of the following and write:

*Your local state or provincial legislator.*

*The governor of your state or premier of your province.*

*The director of your state or province's department of natural resources or related environmental agency.*

On issues concerning federal legislation or to express your opinion about actions taken by the federal government, you can write to:

*Your state's two U.S. senators.*
>The Honorable _____
>U.S. Senate
>Washington, DC 20510

*Your local congressman.*
>The Honorable _____
>U.S. House of Representatives
>Washington, DC 20515

*Your local provincial or federal member of Parliament.*
>The Honorable _____
>House of Commons
>Ottawa, Ontario, Canada K1A 0A6

*The President of the United States.* He has the power to veto, or turn down, bills approved by the Senate and the House of Representatives as well as to introduce bills of his own.
>President _____
>The White House
>1600 Pennsylvania Avenue, NW
>Washington, DC 20501

*The Prime Minister of Canada.*
>The Honorable _____
>House of Commons
>Ottawa, Ontario, Canada K1A 0A6

## Support Organizations

Many national organizations concerned with the environment view controlling population growth as a major factor in preserving a quality environment on our planet. Write for information and find out more about what they do. Here are some suggestions:

Environmental Defense Fund, 257 Park Ave. South, New York, NY 10010

National Audubon Society, 666 Pennsylvania Ave., SE, Washington, DC 20003

National Wildlife Federation, 1412 16th St., NW, Washington, DC 20036

Natural Resources Defense Council, 40 W. 20th St., New York, NY 10011

Planned Parenthood Federation of America, 810 7th Ave., New York, NY 10019

Population Crisis Committee, 1120 19th St., NW, Suite 550, Washington, DC 20036

Population-Environment Balance, 1325 G St., NW, Suite 1003, Washington, DC 20005

Population Institute, 110 Maryland Ave., NE, Washington, DC 20036

Population Reference Bureau, 1875 Connecticut Ave., NW, Suite 520, Washington, DC 20009

Sierra Club, 730 Polk Street, San Francisco, CA 94109

United Nations Population Fund, 220 E. 42nd St., New York, NY 10017

World Population Society, 1333 H St., NW, Washington, DC 20005

Worldwatch Institute, 1776 Massachusetts Ave., NW, Washington, DC 20036

Zero Population Growth, 1400 16th St., NW, 3rd Floor, Washington, DC 20036

Werner Fornos of the Population Institute wrote, "How the human species will treat life on Earth so as to shape our legacies—good or bad—for all time to come will be settled during most of our lifetimes. The responsibility lies squarely with us. Will future generations praise our foresight or look back in anger and dismay at what we had and lost forever?"

# GLOSSARY

**abortion** – the deliberate stopping of a pregnancy by removing the embryo (fertilized egg) from a woman's uterus.

**birth control** – voluntarily preventing pregnancy through the use of contraceptives, abortion, sterilization, not having sexual intercourse, or waiting to marry.

**birth rate** – the number of births per 1,000 people each year. It is found by dividing the number of births by the estimate of population at midyear.

**carrying capacity** – the population of a species, plant and animal, that a particular region or habitat can support year after year without any environmental harm to that region or habitat.

**census** – an official counting of the population, or a specific group within a population, usually done periodically.

**contraception** – the prevention of pregnancy by any means.

**death rate** – the number of deaths per 1,000 people each year. It is found by dividing the number of deaths by the estimate of population at midyear.

**Debt-for-Nature** – a program used by various environmental organizations to help developing nations conserve valuable natural areas and reduce foreign debt. A portion of the foreign debt is reduced if a particular region or habitat is protected from environmental damage.

**deforestation** – cutting down or burning the trees and other plant life of a forest. This process eliminates trees needed to protect against global warming and increases global warming by releasing carbon dioxide, methane, and other greenhouse gases into the atmosphere.

**demographer** – a person who studies human population and its characteristics, such as size, growth, birth and death rates, and global distribution.

**demographic transition** – the period of time it takes for a declining birth rate to equal a declining death rate so that the population becomes stable or slow-growing.

**developed countries** – the industrialized nations of the world such as the United States, Canada, Japan, and the countries in Western Europe.

**developing countries** – poor countries of the world that are trying to develop industries. Also called Third World countries. Some of the poorest countries are called least developed countries.

**environmental degradation** – pollution of air, land, and water so that it no longer safely supports plant, animal, or human use.

**family planning** – personal choices made by men and women to decide if, how, or when they will have children through contraception. Family planning must take place if population growth is to be limited.

**food chain** – the flow of nutrients and energy through a series of living organisms. The first link, the producer, is eaten by a consumer, which in turn may be eaten by a second-level consumer.

**fossil fuels** – coal, oil (petroleum), and natural gas, which were formed from the fossilized remains of ancient organisms. When fossil fuels are burned, they give off carbon dioxide and pollutants of several types.

**gene** – a piece of DNA, usually a protein, that carries the trait for a function or structure in the heredity of a plant or animal.

**gene erosion** – the gradual dying out of varieties of wild plants, causing the disappearance (extinction) of genetic material in their seeds. Modern development techniques such as deforestation, clearing land for agriculture and housing, and overgrazing—especially in developing countries—destroy many plant varieties that might have been useful in the future.

**global warming** – the gradual increase in the planet's temperature caused by an increase in the greenhouse gases in the atmosphere. Not all scientists agree that global warming is occurring.

**Green Revolution** – the rapid growth of modern agricultural methods beginning in the 1970s. Crops were developed that were uniform, and could be grown quickly and in large quantities.

**greenhouse effect** – the trapping of the sun's heat by certain gases, such as carbon dioxide, in the atmosphere, causing the Earth's average temperature to be higher than it would otherwise be.

**greenhouse gas** – any of the gases that contribute to the greenhouse effect, including carbon dioxide, methane, nitrous oxide, ozone, and CFCs. They are molecules that are made up of at least three atoms.

**growth rate** – the birth rate minus the death rate. The closer the growth rate is to zero, the more stable (slower growing) a population is. Sometimes immigration is included in a country's growth rate.

**hybrid** – the offspring of two varieties of plants or animals. Each species may have desirable characteristics that can be combined into a hybrid possessing all desirable characteristics.

**immigration** – people from one country moving to another country permanently.

**infant mortality rate** – the number of newborn babies under the age of 1 year that die per 1,000 live births each year. The mortality rate is especially high for infants of teenage mothers.

**insecticide** – a chemical substance used to kill specific insects.

**lifespan** – the average number of years the people in a population live.

**malnourishment** – improper diet caused from having too little food or not enough of the right kinds of food.

**monsoon** – wind systems that influence the climate of a particular region by changing direction during different seasons. In India, the monsoon brings a dry season and a wet season.

**pesticide** – any chemical substance used to kill any pests, such as weeds, fungi, insects, or rodents.

**refugee** – a person who flees his/her native country or region because of war, lack of food, or denial of human rights.

**stable population** – population that has a growth rate approaching zero

**sterilization** – a method of permanent contraception, usually involving a medical procedure such as tubal ligation, vasectomy, or hysterectomy.

**subsistence farming** – farming at a level that provides only enough food for the farmer's own family, leaving none available for sale.

**sustainable** – able to supply society's current needs without affecting the ability to meet future needs. Sustainable development of natural resources is a goal of most environmentalists.

**topsoil** – the top, most fertile layer of soil.

**total fertility rate** – the average number of live births women have during their lifetimes.

**urbanization** – the process of becoming a city, or the growth of cities in a country. In most countries, the population is moving from rural areas to urbanized areas.

**zero population growth (ZPG)** – slowing population growth rate to—or close to—zero.

# INDEX

**Bold numbers**=illustration

**A**
abortion 81, 122
abortion pill 82
absolute number 21
abundance 107
acid rain 56, 104
Afghans 10
Africa 7, 9, 24, 30, 34, 37, 38, 40, **63**, **68**, 69
agriculture 40, 47, 64, 100
Ahlburg, Dennis 107
AIDS 78
air pollution 12, 54, **55**, 104
algae 44
Amazon 62
anti-pregnancy vaccine 81
arithmetic progression 25
Armageddon 117
Asia 7, 37, 40
Asilomar Declaration for Sustainable Agriculture 102
Asimov, Isaac 54
atmosphere 111

**B**
baby boomers 7
back alley abortions 82
Bailey, Ronald 108
Bangladesh **34**, 61, **67**, **109**
barley 40
biological fallacy 108
birth control 75, 76, **89**, 122
birth rate 8, 19, 23, 24, 88, **95**, 107, 122
Black Death 17
Borlaug, Norman 45
boys, preferred over girls 92, 94
brain development 35
Brazil 53, **54**, **56**, 103
bubonic plague 17

**C**
California 64
Canada 8, 22, 80, 84, 86, 102, 104, 118
Capronar 78
carbon dioxide 56, 60
Caribbeans 10
carrying capacity 99, 122
cars 12, 27, 28, 55, **60**, **64**, 67, 97, 113
Carter, President Jimmy 26
cash 40, 70
cassava 35
cattle **47**
census 15, 122
cervical cap 78

124

Chicago 17
child care 41, **83**
child labor **71**
children, numbers of 21, 73
children, selling 30
China 10, **12**, **14**, **19**, 36, 63, 78, 81, **91**, 92
cities 23, 31, 53, 69
Club of Rome 26
coal 27, 28, 57, 68
colonial nations 112
Commoner, Barry 111
communications 59
conception 76
condoms 77-79, 90, 92
Constitution 82
consumer goods 59, 102
contraception 76, 122
contraceptive sponges 79
contraceptives 77, 90
corn 36, 40-42
corn-leaf blight 42
corporations 112
crop yields 40

**D**
DDT 66
death from starvation 33, **34**
death rate 20, 22, 122
Debt-for-Nature 100, 122
deforestation **27**, 54, **57**, 60, 62, 63, 100, 122
dehydration 33
demographers 15, 113, 122
demographic transition 23, 24, 122
developed countries 10, 70, 102, 104, 122
developing countries 7, 22, **23**, 24, 66, 70, **75**, 85, 100, 102, 104, 122
diaphragm 78
*Diet for a Small Planet* 46, 115
disease 22, 33, 88
disease resistance 40
disease, sexually transmitted 78

drought 10, **22**, **36**, **37**, 110
Durning, Alan 67

**E**
Earth Day 26
Earth Summit 103
economic development 73, 74, 89, 97, 108
ecosphere 111
education 9, 12, 74, 85, 88, 91, 93, **94**
egg 82
Egypt 37
Ehrlich, Anne H. 13, 27
Ehrlich, Dr. Paul 13, 26, 27, 59, 107, 108, 111
electric power 60
electricity 28, 67
embryo 81, 84
energy 102
energy in food 47
energy sources 67
energy use 44
England 118
environment 29, 54, 95, 97, 104, 113, 115
environmental costs 112
environmental degradation 67, **93**, 122
environmental disasters 10
Environmental Impact 59
Ethiopia **10**, **30**, 62
Europe 10, 80
Experiences 18, 28, 31, 35, 38, 46, 98, 116

**F**
Fallopian tubes 80
family planning 72, **76**, **79**, 85, **91**, 122
family planning, arguments against 85
family size 74, **81**
famine 10, **12**, 34, 42, 76
farming 102, **109**
farmland 66

fertility awareness 77
fertilizers 39, 40, **41**, 44, 47, 54
fetus 84
fish 43
flooding 10
food chain 47, 48, 115, 122
food distribution **50**
food supply 9, 12, **49**, 109
food wasting 45
Ford Foundation 40
forests 9, 62
Fornos, Werner 117, 121
fossil fuels 27, 44, **45**, 47, 55-57, 60, 67, 122
France 82
Fremlin, J. H. 25
fuelwood 30, 62, 73

**G**
gene 122
gene banks 100, **101**
gene erosion 42, 100, 122
geometric progression 25
Germany 22, 102
Ghana **23**, 34, **43**, **63**, 89
girls, missing in China 92
*Global 2000 Report to the President of the United States* 26
global warming 27, 56, **58**, 60, 66, 123
government 75
grains 40, 46
Great Britain 82
Great Depression 7
Green Revolution 40, **41**, 45, 100, 108, 123
greenhouse effect 57, 123
greenhouse gas 123
growth rate 13, 20, 23, 123
growth, stunted 36

**H**
Han people of China 12
harvest 30, **45**
health care **10**, 74, **83**, 87, 93
health-care workers 85, 87

125

Hong Kong **110**
hormone 78-79
Hungary 20
hunger 36
hunger, death from 13
hybrid **41**, 42, 123
hydrosphere 111

**I**
immigration 7, 8, **21**, 43, 123
income 73
India **2**, 20, 37, 40, **85**, 92, **93**
Indonesia 40, 62, **78**, 87, **99**
industrial development **23**, 70, 112
Industrial Revolution 23
industrialization **93**, 98, 101, 103, **111**
industrialized countries 10, 22, 54, 66, 67, 76
infant mortality 30
infant mortality rate **86**, 87, 93, 123
insecticide 123
intelligence 108, 113
International Conference on Population 74
intra-uterine device 79
Iran **65**, 87
Ireland 43
irrigation 37, 40, **43**, 44, 47, 64, 65, 99, **100**
Israel 21
Italy 86
IUD 79, 81

**J**
Japan 20, 22, **59**, **81**, 102
jobs, in Third World countries 28

**K**
Kenya **9**, 12, 31, **76**, **79**, 85
kwashiorkor **34**

**L**
land 63, 68, 109
land degradation 54
landfill **68**
land loss 64
Lappé, Frances Moore 46, 115
Latin America 10, 40, **49**, 88
lifespan 20, 123
*Limits to Growth* 26
living standard 25

**M**
mahogany 62
*Making Peace with the Planet* 111
malaria 20
malnourishment **34**, **36**, 123
Malthus, Thomas R. 24, 26, 107, 108, 109
Malthusian Leagues 25
meats 47
medicine 20
Mediterranean Sea 104
menstrual periods 77
Mexico City **55**
Middle East 26
migration **9**, 53
millet 40
miscarriage 81
monsoons **37**, 123
Mozambique 10
Muslims **86**

**N**
National Academy of Sciences 26
natural gas 27, 57
Netherlands 118
Nigeria 88
Nobel Peace Prize 45
nonrenewable resources 99
Norplant 78
North America 10, 36, 39
Northern Hemisphere 70
nuclear power 68, 112
nutrition 88
Nyerere, Dr. Julius 71

**O**
oil 26, 27, 57, 107
one-child law 91
Organization of Economic Cooperation and Development 101
organizations 120
ovaries 80
ovulation 77-78
ozone 55, 123
ozone layer 97

**P**
Palestinians 10
parental permission 82
per capita income 108
pesticides **41**, 43, 44, 47, 65, 66, 113, 123
photosynthesis 47
Pill 78, 79
plague 76
poisons 66
pollutants 27, 112
pollution 26, 54, 66, 68, **93**, 101, 110, **111**
polygamy **24**
population 7, 10, 13, 97
*Population Bomb* 26
population control 75
population doubling 17
*Population Explosion* 27
population explosion 26, 98
population forecasts 9, 24
population growth 8, 13, **16**, 22, 76, 89, 94
Population Institute 117, 121
population limit 25
population reduction 111
population stabilization 66, 77, 88, 101
Population-Environment Balance 113
potatoes 35, 43
poverty 9, 69, 98, 101
predictions 107
pregnancy 75, 81, 84

primary consumers  47
producer organisms  47
protein  34, 35, 43, 46

**R**
radio  59
rain forest  53, 54, 100
recycling  102
recycling by nature  68, 112
refugees  **10**, 33, **61**, 123
religious opinion  77, 86
replacement level  91
reservoir  65
resources  8, 75, 105, 109
resources, imbalance  68, 70
rhythm method  77, 86
rice  **37**, 40, **41**, 43
Rienow, Robert and Leona  45
Rockefeller Foundation  40
*Roe vs. Wade*  82
Roman Catholic Church  77, 86
RU-486  82

**S**
Sadik, Nafis  13
salinization  **65**, 99, 123
salts  65
sanitation  88
secondary consumers  47
sexual intercourse  75, 76
shrimp  43
Simon, Julian  108
Singapore  89
slums  69
smog  27
soap opera  88
soil  54, 62, 65
solar energy  111
South America  7

South Commission  71
Southern Hemisphere  70, 71
Soviet republics  36
Soviet Union  21, 90
soybeans  46
sperm  80
Sri Lanka  20, 42
stabilization of population  66, 77, 88, 101
stable population  123
standard of living  70
starvation  33
sterilization  79, 87, 123
stockholders  112
subsistence farming  25, 39, **54**, 73, 123
sugarcane  44
sustainability  96
sustainable  97, **105**, 115, 123
Sweden  118

**T**
taxes  75
technology  60, 70, 99, 110, **113**
technosphere  111
teenage pregnancy  84, 118
teenagers  82, 84, 117, **118**
television  59
television shows  88
Thailand  92
Third World  26
Third World countries  7, 27, 38, 40, 66, 69, 70, 94
topsoil  27, **38**, 62, **63**, 123
total fertility rate  21, **86**, 122
tubal ligation  80

**U**
U.S. Supreme Court  82, 84
ultimate resource  108

United Nations  9, 15, 66, 74, 95, 107
United Nations Conference on Environment and Development  103
United Nations Population Fund  13, 79, 89
United States  7, 8, 15, 21, 22, 31, 36, 37, 43, 45, 66, 67, 77, 80, 82, 86, 89, 102, 104, 112, 118
urbanization  **49**, **68**, 69, 123
uterus  78, 81

**V**
vaginal ring  79
vasectomy  80
Viravaidya, Mechai  92

**W**
war  76, 97, 110, 112, **113**
water projects  44, **65**
water resources  9, 12, 68
water supplies  **8**, **13**, **37**, 30, 43, 54, 62, 63, 97, 113
water table  63
weather  37
wheat  36, 40, 44
women, status of  **30**, 34, **73-75**, **83**, 91, 93
World Bank  9
World Health Organization  79, 84
World War II  7

**Z**
Zero Population Growth  68, 77, 80
zero population growth (ZPG)  20, 123

127

## PHOTO SOURCES

Agricultural Research Service, USDA: 101 (top)
Air India Library: 93
American Petroleum Institute: 96, 102
Dr. Howard W. Barnes: 14, 15, 19, 45 (right), 103 (top)
Dr. Gary Benson: 24, 68 (right), 90
Margie Benson: 83 (bottom right & left), 118
Brazil Tourism Office: 56
California Department of Water Resources: 100, 105
State of California/Department of Transportation: 60
Cenex/Land O' Lakes Agricultural Services: 41 (top left, bottom left)
Courtesy of the Danish Tourist Board: 95
S.C. Delaney/EPA: 68 (left)
Food & Agriculture Organization/B. Rouget: 37 (right)
Food & Agriculture Organization/F. Botts: 34 (right)
Food & Agriculture Organization/F. Mattioli: 13, 22, 50 (left), 54, 87, 103 (bottom)
Food & Agriculture Organization/Fiona McDougall: 47 (right)
Food & Agriculture Organization/J. VanAcker: 50 (right)
Food & Agriculture Organization/M. Cherry: 63, 99
Food & Agriculture Organization/P. McCloskey: 65 (right)
Food & Agriculture Organization/Peyton Johnson: 43 (right), 47 (right), 109 (left)
Owen Franken/German Information Center: 106
Carrol Henderson: 101 (bottom)
Jeanine Hess: 83 (top right)
Hong Kong Tourist Association: 110
Industry, Science & Technology Canada-Riceton, Saskatchewan: 45 (left)
International Development Association: 85
International Planned Parenthood Federation: 89
Japan National Tourist Organization: 59, 81
Dr. Stephen P. Leatherman, Laboratory for Coastal Research, University of Maryland at College Park: 58
Jed Maker, M.D.: 83 (top left)
Beth Mittermaier: 41 (top right)
National Aeronautics & Space Administration: 18
Padilla Bay National Estuarine Research Reserve: 71 (left)
John Snow Inc.: 79
Soil Conservation Service: 41 (bottom right), 52
South Coast Air Quality Management District: 64
Jeri Spangler: 114
Dr. Louis Uehling: 21, 38, 55
UNICEF Photo Library: 6
United Nations 108508: 27
United Nations 125271/J. Robaton: 32
United Nations 131279/J. P. Laffont: 104
United Nations 132561: 16, 17
United Nations 133250/Carl Purcell: 8
United Nations 139456/J. Foxx: 75
United Nations 141453/J. K. Isaac: 61
United Nations 146122/O. Monsen: 9
United Nations 148001/J. P. Laffont: 71 (right)
United Nations 148007/J.P. Laffont: 53
United Nations 151512/J. K. Isaac: 74
United Nations 152454/Ian Steele: 30
United Nations 152582: 2
United Nations 152739: 91
United Nations 153444: 83 (middle)
United Nations 153703/J. K. Isaac: 37 (left)
United Nations 153762/J. K. Isaac: 72
United Nations 154780/J. K. Isaac: 73
United Nations 156592: 86
United Nations 157068: 67
United Nations 157625: 57
United Nations 158181: 113
United Nations 164600/J. K. Isaac: 36
United Nations/Ray Witlin: 65 (left)
United States Department of Housing and Urban Development: 108, 111
UNRRA Photo released by FAO: 12
World Bank Photo Library: 10, 23, 34 (left), 41 (middle), 43 (left), 49, 76, 78, 94 (both), 109 (right)

## ABOUT THE AUTHORS

Jean F. Blashfield and Wallace B. Black are dedicated environmentalists, writers, and publishers who are responsible for this book and the *SAVING PLANET EARTH* series. Working together, with other environmentalists, educators, and Childrens Press, they have developed 13 other books in the *SAVING PLANET EARTH* series.

This creative team was responsible for the creation of *THE YOUNG PEOPLE'S SCIENCE ENCYCLOPEDIA* and *ABOVE AND BEYOND, THE ENCYCLOPEDIA OF AVIATION AND SPACE SCIENCES*. In addition, Jean Blashfield was the editor-in-chief of *THE YOUNG STUDENTS ENCYCLOPEDIA* and is the author of more than 25 other books. Wallace Black, a former pilot in the United States Air Force, is the author of a series of books on World War II.